John has done it again! Another in a great collection of classics, only this time, the reader takes center stage as *X: Multiply Your God-Given Potential* helps the reader uncover what so many are searching for— their purpose. So many books talk about potential but few have the ability to take you, step-by-step, through a process that not only helps you discover what you were created to do, but what you can do today to move in that direction. John is a masterful teacher, and this book is a much-needed resource for every church discipleship ministry and for believers who know they were made for more.

> JENTEZEN FRANKLIN
> Senior Pastor of Free Chapel
> *New York Times* best-selling author

Your potential is not automatic; it must be developed. My friend John Bevere provides the spark you need to rise above complacency and boldly pursue your destiny!

> MARK BATTERSON
> *New York Times* best-selling author of *The Circle Maker*
> Lead Pastor of National Community Church

John Bevere's book *X: Multiply Your God-Given Potential* is more than a book on discovering your purpose. It's a manual for discovering your gifts, living a God-honoring life, and investing in others. If you are passionate about making a difference, this book is one to read and reread for years to come!

> CRAIG GROESCHEL
> Pastor of Life.Church
> *New York Times* best-selling author

This book is for the doers—the people who are ready to step up and step out in the pursuit of their God-given potential. It's not an easy journey, but this book may be just what you need to help you along the way.

> STEVEN FURTICK
> Pastor of Elevation Church
> *New York Times* best-selling author

I firmly believe each one of us was created with a specific individual purpose as well as a shared purpose—to build the Kingdom of God. *X: Multiply Your God-Given Potential* will help you identify your specific individual purpose and discover how you can multiply that to build God's Kingdom.

> CHRISTINE CAINE
> Best-selling author
> Founder of A21 and Propel Women

I love this book! Author and friend John Bevere has written a masterpiece that is sure to inspire countless numbers of believers to step into their God-given design and potential. This possibility excites me beyond words. He shares from his own experiences how he stepped past his own skill level into a realm of grace, that he might see what God would do through him. And the outcome is brilliant.

John inspires us to push past our comfort zones into the realm of advancement, where we see the manifestation of God's will on the earth through the power of multiplication. The insights and inspiration contained on these pages is worth the book's weight in gold. I sincerely believe that *X: Multiply Your God-Given Potential* will contribute to the reformation we all long for. Let us steward our God-given potential with such faithfulness that, at the end of our days, we may stand before Him and hear Him say, "Well done, good and faithful servant."

BILL JOHNSON
Senior Leader of Bethel Church
Author of *The Way of Life* and *Strengthen Yourself in the Lord*

To reach your potential, you must grow. And to grow, you must be highly intentional about it. My friend John Bevere has penned an incredible book that gives you the tools to both accelerate your growth and realize your potential.

JOHN MAXWELL
Best-selling author and leadership expert

What God has placed within you is too valuable to remain buried and hidden by fear. John was catalytic in helping me discover and realize my potential. I know these truths will help do the same for you!

LISA BEVERE
New York Times best-selling author
Co-founder of Messenger International

JOHN BEVERE

BESTSELLING AUTHOR OF *THE BAIT OF SATAN*

**MULTIPLY YOUR
GOD-GIVEN POTENTIAL**

X: Multiply Your God-Given Potential
© 2020 by John P. Bevere

Published by Messenger International
610 South Santa Fe Ridge
Palmer Lake, CO 80133

www.MessengerInternational.org

Printed in the United States of America

ISBN 978-1-937558-25-3 (hardcover edition)
ISBN 978-1-937558-26-0 (paperback edition)
ISBN 978-1-937558-24-6 (electronic edition)

LCCN: 2020938665

Unless otherwise indicated, all Scripture quotations are taken from the Holy Bible, New Living Translation, copyright © 1996, 2004, 2015 by Tyndale House Foundation. Used by permission of Tyndale House Publishers, a Division of Tyndale House Ministries, Carol Stream, Illinois 60188. All rights reserved. Scripture quotations marked AMPC are taken from the Amplified Bible Classic Edition, copyright © 1954, 1958, 1962, 1964, 1965, 1987 by The Lockman Foundation. Scripture quotations marked ESV are from The ESV® Bible (The Holy Bible, English Standard Version®), copyright © 2001 by Crossway, a publishing ministry of Good News Publishers. Used by permission. All rights reserved. Scripture quotations marked MSG are taken from THE MESSAGE, copyright © 1993, 2002, 2018 by Eugene H. Peterson. Used by permission of NavPress. All rights reserved. Represented by Tyndale House Publishers, a Division of Tyndale House Ministries. Scripture quotations marked NKJV are taken from the New King James Version®. Copyright © 1982 by Thomas Nelson. Used by permission. All rights reserved. Scripture quotations marked NCV are taken from the New Century Version®. Copyright © 2005 by Thomas Nelson. Used by permission. All rights reserved. Scripture quotations marked TPT are from The Passion Translation®. Copyright © 2017, 2018 by Passion & Fire Ministries, Inc. Used by permission. All rights reserved. ThePassionTranslation.com. Scripture quotations marked GNT are from the Good News Translation in Today's English Version–Second Edition. Copyright © 1992 by American Bible Society. Used by permission. Except in quotations from the *Amplified Bible*, any italicizations or words in brackets added to Scripture quotations are the author's additions for emphasis or clarity.

Edited by Bruce Nygren, Chris Pace, and Cory Emberson.

Cover design by Allan Nygren.

SPECIAL MARKET SALES
Organizations, churches, pastors, and small group leaders can receive special discounts when purchasing this book and other resources from John Bevere. For more information, please call (800) 648-1477 or send an email to orders@messengerinternational.org.

Dedicated to the magnificent wives of our sons . . .

Lisa and I love you deeply and each of you
exhibits the beautiful traits listed below and more,
but these are the ones that stand out the most:

Julianna
Married to Addison October 25, 2009.
You are lovely and wise.
You will always be my first daughter.

Jessica
Married to Austin September 24, 2018.
You are kind and adorable.
Joy fills the atmosphere wherever you go.

Christian
Married to Arden November 18, 2018.
You are full of grace and tender of heart.
You love our son beautifully.

The future Mrs. Alec Bevere
My heart longs to meet our future daughter.
I love you deeply already.

Each of you brings great joy to Lisa and me.
Thank you for multiplying our family.
Forever our daughters.

CONTENTS

ABOUT THIS BOOK

Throughout these pages, you'll find biblical insights and strategies that will empower you to discover your purpose, ignite your passion, and realize your potential. With each chapter, there are also reflective questions that will help you personalize what you're learning.

If you'd like to learn more about how to multiply, I've created bonus content, including video lessons, a companion guide, and other online resources that can be used individually or in a group setting. You can access these resources, along with my entire library of discipleship resources, at **www.MessengerX.com**. Millions of people have used our resources, and our goal is to make them available to every person, regardless of their location, language, or financial position (something you'll learn more about in this book). Take a minute to check out the site and join our global community of messengers.

And if you have any questions, please don't hesitate to reach out to me and my team at Messenger International.

Cheering you on!
John

Scan the QR code to download MessengerX

Fear of the LORD is the foundation of wisdom. . . . Wisdom will multiply your days and add years to your life. If you become wise, you will be the one to benefit.

—Proverbs 9:10–12

1

Connecting
the Dots

The year was 2012. I was scheduled to speak in the Los Angeles area for a church's weekend services. My normal pattern is to fly in late Saturday afternoon, minister Saturday evening and Sunday morning, and return home Sunday afternoon. This routine was about to change.

One of our ministry partners, I'll call him Stan, in discovering I was scheduled in the LA area, called and asked if I would like to play the golf course at the famous Riviera Country Club. I didn't have to think twice, as playing this course was on my bucket list. I enthusiastically responded, "Absolutely yes, I'd love to!"

Let me give some backstory. In over thirty-five years of traveling and communicating God's Word, every once in a while, my love for playing golf slips out when addressing audiences. An unplanned, yet pleasant outcome over the years has been several offers to play some of the nicest golf clubs in the world. This certainly was such an occasion.

This was a *very special* invitation. Riviera is an exclusive and private club—very difficult to get into. Each year this course hosts the PGA tour event called the Genesis Invitational (formerly known as the Los Angeles Open). It has also hosted major tournaments, including a few US Opens, PGA Championships, the US Amateur, and other notable tournaments.

Stan picked me up early Saturday morning for the dream round. To make matters even sweeter, one of my close friends, Aaron Baddeley, had just won the LA Open the year before. I anticipated mentally replaying some of his outstanding shots from winning the tournament in 2011!

I started out the first four holes being three over par (nerves got the best of me), but ended the round at two under par. Stan and I had a great time together; it was a memorable morning, to say the least.

On the drive back to my hotel in downtown Los Angeles, Stan asked a heartfelt question: "John, can I ask you about an issue I've been wrestling with?"

"Sure."

In a vulnerable and most sincere manner, he set up his question: "John, I've worked tirelessly and diligently, giving many hours to build my businesses over the past couple of decades. My net worth is now approximately $9 million. Everything is running smoothly with my current clients. The result of years of hard work is that my wife and children are financially set for life."

Then came his question: "Now that I'm entering the decade of my fifties, why should I work at the same pace? Why should I struggle to build my businesses to $35 million over the next ten years?"

The Holy Spirit instantly gave me wisdom on how to answer. "Let me pose a scenario to you," I said. "Suppose I was to say to you, 'Stan, I've spent years working hard to write seventeen books that are now in over eighty languages with copies numbering in the multiple millions. I've flown over ten million miles in the past twenty-five years, fought jet lag, experienced a variety of cultures and strange foods, and stayed in tiny hotel rooms—all to be able to minister the gospel all over the globe. The ministry is doing well and finances are stable; Lisa and my children are set, too. Why should I continue to work at this same rate?'"

It was a perfect setup. With a slight chuckle, he answered, "I wouldn't want to be in your shoes when you face Jesus one day."

I immediately said, "Stan, that's exactly what you said to me in regard to your businesses."

The smile immediately left his face. He turned his eyes away from the highway toward me with a look of shock. In disbelief he questioned, "How do you get that?"

"Stan, God has gifted every one of His children. These gifts are divinely given to build His kingdom. However, we are stewards and therefore can choose, at any given time, to use these gifts in one of three ways:

"We can use the gifts to build the kingdom.

"We can use the gifts to build ourselves.

"We can just neglect the gifts altogether."

I had Stan's attention, so I continued: "Some of my obvious gifts are writing and speaking; your gifts are related to business and giving. You just laughed at my scenario! However, your scenario is exactly the same. Your gifts are just as important for building the kingdom as mine are. In fact, yours may be more important, but you haven't connected the dots!"

We continued to talk along these lines. From our conversation, it was both fulfilling and enjoyable to see the rapid change in Stan's thoughts and attitude.

Six months later, I called Stan to touch base and see how he was. It was another unforgettable chat.

"Hey, Stan, how you doing?"

"Do you want the honest truth?" His answer caught me off guard.

"Yes, of course!"

"I've been haunted, in a good way, over the words you spoke to me six months ago."

"What are you doing about it?"

With a laugh, he quickly stated, "I'm busting my rear end to build my businesses up to $35 million for the sake of building the kingdom."

"Good for you!"

Stan had grasped the reality that he's not a spectator in advancing God's kingdom, but a vital participant. He'd caught the vision, which eludes so many, that his unique abilities are valuable for the eternal, not just the temporal. Now he fully understands he's gifted for a greater purpose than himself and his family. I'm so grateful he was blunt, sincere, and humble. These traits opened him up to receive the truth that would change his life. And, due to his testimony, not only his life but, in turn, so many others.

Stan's enlightenment has now become his motivation to multiply and exemplifies the primary purpose of this book. In conversing with believers throughout my years of travel, the vast number who think no differently than Stan is a shocking reality. In fact, if I were backed into a corner, I would have to say it's the majority. However, many are not as forthright as Stan in admitting it, but as conversations ensue, the disconnect is uncovered.

If you question your purpose with similar thoughts, I'm so happy you have this book in your hands. It's my sincere hope your paradigm will also shift.

As with Stan, be honest with yourself; it will help connect your dots. In this posture of humility, you'll discover and firmly believe in multiplying your unique gifts for building the kingdom. You are just as called by God as your pastor or I. Your calling is as legitimate as was that of the great Billy Graham or any other well-known minister.

We will discuss how to discover, develop and, most importantly, multiply your gifts to enhance your specific calling. The Word of God and the stories contained in this book will build your faith to greatly increase your effectiveness. I know firsthand; it happened with me as I typed and edited this book.

BORN ON PURPOSE FOR A PURPOSE

Let's begin by examining a very familiar portion of Scripture:

> For by *grace* you have been saved through faith, and that not of yourselves; it is *the gift of God*, not of works, lest anyone should boast. (Ephesians 2:8–9 NKJV)

The focus of these two verses is the *grace of God*. It is clear—abundantly clear—that we are saved by grace and this is a gift from God. The twenty-first-century church has done an excellent job of communicating this truth. We can never work hard, live pure, or sacrifice enough to earn the privilege of spending eternity with our Creator, Almighty God. This familiar scripture has been one of the—if not the primary—references to reveal this important truth. However, there has been neglect in what comes next:

> *For* we are His workmanship, created in Christ Jesus for good works, which God prepared beforehand that we *should* walk in them. (Ephesians 2:10 NKJV)

Notice that the next word after the ninth verse is *for*. This word is a *conjunction*, which joins the two statements together. In other words, the beginning of the thought is not complete on its own. The word *for* means "because of this," so verse 10 should not be left out when citing verses 8 and 9; otherwise you don't get the complete meaning of what's being communicated.

Verse 10 states that we are His handiwork created for a purpose—to produce good works. So, in essence, in these three verses Paul is saying:

> We are saved by grace *to first be someone*—a child of God; *and*
> we are equally empowered by that same grace *to do something.*

We can never overemphasize one truth to the neglect of another truth. But let me emphasize up front that who we are in Christ Jesus is paramount to what we do, for *anything we do should be an outflow of who we are.*

It is easy to shy away from the "to-do something" aspect, as it relieves us from any pressure of laboring to build the kingdom. The sad reality is, though, that it's our labor that energizes us. Jesus says, "My food is to do the will of Him who sent Me, and to finish His work" (John 4:34 NKJV). He also says, "As the Father has sent Me, I also send you" (John 20:21 NKJV). Putting His two statements together, we clearly see that our food is to do and finish the will of Jesus who sends us. Food is what strengthens us. If we don't eat, we become weak and are good for very little.

Let's now bring this over to our spiritual life. If we don't do the will of Jesus who sends us, we become weak. Now we are vulnerable to temptation.

In over forty years of walking with Jesus, I've noticed that one of the primary causes of people slipping away from the faith is a lack of "doing." They become lazy and idle in regard to their calling, and before they know it, they find themselves in complacent drunkenness, immorality, or given to interests that pull them back into the world's way of living. They lose their spiritual strength. Here's the bottom line:

What we do strengthens us.

So, allow me to restate the truth of these three Scriptures: You were born again by the free gift of grace to be a child of God, and you were equally empowered by that same grace to do something. Scripture declares God planned each of our works beforehand. David writes:

> You saw me before I was born. Every day of my life was re-
> corded in Your book. Every moment was laid out before a
> single day had passed. (Psalm 139:16)

God designed things for you to do before you were born. He actually recorded these works in a book! We can only imagine how huge this book is, because every moment of our life is recorded in it. These assignments He planned for us revolve around building His kingdom. It's His deepest desire that we fulfill His plans for our life, but it is not guaranteed that we will. Notice in Ephesians 2:10 the word *should*. It doesn't say "that we *would* walk in them," rather "that we *should* walk in them." Here is where our free will enters the game. He prearranged our works, but it is up to us to walk in what He planned.

I'm firmly convinced that when we stand before Jesus at the believer's judgment seat (where we will be rewarded for our labor as Christians or suffer loss for our neglect), He will open this book and say, "Let's compare how you actually lived to the original plan My Father and I had in mind for you." (In regard to the judgment, it is written in two different places in Scripture that the "books were opened" (see Daniel 7:10 and Revelation 20:12 NKJV).) I believe these books were written by God about our life before we were born. In regard to our specific calling, we won't be judged on what we did, rather on what we were called to do. That's sobering.

At this point you may feel a little panic. Please don't! There are three important things to note: First, God is more passionate about you completing what He's called you to do than you are, so He's not going to hide His plans from you. He desires for you to know your calling more than you want to! Second, the process of growing into the fullness of your calling is a journey, not a one-time event, so fight the urge to give in to impatience. Third, in this book you'll find insights from both Scripture and experience in order to discover and develop your calling.

To help illustrate, consider this example. Suppose I am a city planner and desire to build a spectacular residential, recreational, and retail shop complex near the city center. Being the city planner makes me the chief designer, so I organize the master plan with skilled developers and architects. In this complex I want play areas, amusement rides, sports courts, fountains, sitting areas, and walking trails. I also want to incorporate retail shops with upstairs condominiums, restaurants, movie theaters, and other creative accents to make our complex unique.

Once the design is complete, I then determine what contractors I will need to accomplish the different aspects of the master plan. I hire these various contractors and give the time line for their assignments. The project is set to commence.

If all the contractors do exactly what I ask, the massive project will be built seamlessly and run smoothly. However, what if some of the contractors don't make this project a priority? What if they accept the assignment but, in the allotted time for construction, use their skills to work on other jobs? What if they go fishing, golfing, and attend sporting events too often so the job gets neglected? What if others are lazy and don't take their work seriously? If I totally depend on these original contractors, the project wouldn't get done on schedule. In fact, it may never be done.

The choice belongs to the contractors in what to do with their time and talents. However, as the city planner, I'm not going to settle for major delays or the possibility of the project never being finished. Instead, I'm going to have to bring in others to do the work.

What is the result? The original contractors don't get the reward of being a part of the team that builds the beautiful complex. They will not be able to show their children, grandchildren, and friends their part in the beautiful focus of the city center. Their children will not be able to tell others about what their parents were a part of. They also will lose the reward of being paid for the assignment.

You can see this same principle exemplified all through Scripture. God has a master plan for the building of His kingdom. Yet, throughout history, God has had to work with people who haven't fulfilled His desires. Therefore, He's frequently had to adjust His original plan. (I speak in human terms because God knows the end from the beginning—He's not bound to time.) Therefore, "changing" the plan is not a shock to Him. He knew what His laborers would choose beforehand. He was already prepared with their replacements.

Here are a few of many examples of this in Scripture. You see this with Abraham's father, Terah. (Our youngest son, Arden, recently reminded me of this truth.) Most of us know that Abraham was born and grew up in Ur of the Chaldeans before God called him to go to the land of Canaan. The lesser known fact is that if you look closely at his father, Terah, you'll discover he was more likely the original one called to do this. We read:

One day Terah took his son Abram, his daughter-in-law Sarai (his son Abram's wife), and his grandson Lot (his son Haran's

child) and moved away from Ur of the Chaldeans. He was
headed for the land of Canaan, but they stopped at Haran and
settled there. Terah lived for 205 years and died while still in
Haran. (Genesis 11:31–32)

There are two things to consider. First, why would a man, for no
reason, uproot his family from Ur and travel over six hundred miles
toward, of all places, the land of Canaan? The trip by camel is slow
and arduous. With women and children, it probably took at least a
few months. It's not like Terah could go online and see pictures and
read articles of Canaan being a great place to live and work. He didn't
discover it through posts on social media. There would have to have
been a reason for this distinct and distant move.

Second, if he was headed for Canaan, why did he settle in Haran?
Why didn't he complete his journey to the destination? Could it be
that he was tempted to not finish? Could he have run up against in-
terfering desires, hardships, a family member who was fed up with
traveling, or other distracting circumstances? Could it have been that
he saw more chances for opportunity in Haran and didn't want to risk
losing out on them simply over a word from God?

In considering all this, could we possibly conclude that Terah was
God's first choice to be "the father of many nations"? Was he also originally assigned to be the *father of faith*, a term now ascribed to Abraham (see Romans 4:16–17)?

Terah decided to not go the distance; he settled in Haran. I believe
if he had stayed the course, today we would read about his adventures
and covenant with God. I believe Israel would have ascribed him to
be their father and that Jesus would have been referred to as the "seed
of Terah" instead of the "seed of Abraham" (see Galatians 3:16).

Another example of a change in God's master plan is the judge
and head priest Eli. He and his descendants were assigned to be the

priests who would approach God for the people. However, a prophet sent to Eli declared:

> The LORD, the God of Israel, says: I promised that your branch of the tribe of Levi would always be My priests. But I will honor those who honor Me, and I will despise those who think lightly of Me. The time is coming when I will put an end to your family, so it will no longer serve as My priests. (1 Samuel 2:30–31)

Eli's disobedience affected both him and his descendants. Had he walked honorably before God, the priesthood would have continued with Eli's clan.

Still another example is all the kings of Israel. The first would be David's son Solomon. God said to him, "Since you have not kept My covenant and have disobeyed My decrees, I will surely tear the kingdom away from you and give it to one of your servants" (1 Kings 11:11). Later, had Solomon stayed true, the kingdom never would have been ripped away from his son, Rehoboam. The majority of the kingdom was given to Jeroboam, yet later he also failed in being faithful. God told him:

> I promoted you from the ranks of the common people and made you ruler over My people Israel. I ripped the kingdom away from the family of David and gave it to you. But you have not been like My servant David, who obeyed My commands and followed Me with all his heart and always did whatever I wanted. . . . And since you have turned your back on Me, I will bring disaster on your dynasty. (1 Kings 14:7–10)

Jeroboam would have had an enduring dynasty had he not misused his position and gifts to benefit himself instead of God's kingdom.

A similar message was given to King Baasha of Israel (see 1 Kings 16:1–7), as well as to others entrusted with kingdom responsibilities.

Here's my point: Often our unfaithfulness to the call of God on our life affects not only us, but also our descendants. With Terah it didn't, but with many others it did.

We see a similar situation among the prophets. Elisha served Elijah and received a double portion of what was on Elijah's life. But years later, Elisha's servant, Gehazi, who was next in line to walk in the prophetic gifting, lost focus of what was important and pulled away. He became a leper and left the service he was originally called to (see 2 Kings 5:20–27). A new servant (who was not named) moved into his place to assist Elisha.

In the New Testament you see this with Judas Iscariot. Because he misused his calling and the gifts entrusted to him, he had to be replaced. Peter said to the disciples in the upper room, "This was written in the book of Psalms, where it says, . . . 'Let someone else take his position.' So now we must choose a replacement for Judas" (Acts 1:20–21).

How sad, how tragic! It's sobering to think of the regrets many will have because they chose to not steward the calling or gifts upon their lives in a worthy manner.

In returning to the positive aspect, you, dear reader, were born on purpose and for a purpose. Your life has great value in building the eternal. It's not the will of a mere man or woman, but determined by God Himself.

YOU DETERMINE YOUR EFFECTIVENESS

Here is the startling reality: *How effective you are is not up to God but up to you.* That may sound irreverent if you have put all your life achievements in the basket of "God's sovereignty." I assure you, however, it is not irreverent nor does this statement take anything away from the sovereignty of God. It is a testimony of His trust in us, and His desire for His sons and daughters to exercise the free will He's given us.

Let's look again at a portion of the Scripture that opened this chapter:

Wisdom will *multiply your days* and add years to your life.
If you become wise, you will be the one to benefit. (Proverbs 9:11–12)

This truth is so encouraging and powerful! What does it mean to *multiply your days*? It can't mean to lengthen your life; this is already covered by the statement, ". . . and add years to your life." It can't mean anything other than increasing your effectiveness each and every day. In other words, you'll get more out of the day than someone without God's wisdom.

You've most likely heard the proverb, "If the ax is dull, and one does not sharpen the edge, then he must use more strength; but wisdom brings success" (Ecclesiastes 10:10 NKJV). Wisdom is the focus here. You will not be as effective or productive with a dull ax (a lack of wisdom). Conversely, you'll be able to cut down many more trees with an ax that's sharpened (living wisely). You will multiply your efforts using the same strength.

God's wisdom is so important. I will share a story later in the book of a friend of mine who was unproductive as a believer for decades and eventually became fed up with his lethargic state. The first thing he did was to immerse himself in the Scriptures for six months. This gave him the wisdom to be more effective, and you'll be amazed by his life story.

It's not just my friend, but all of us are told, "Getting wisdom is the most important thing you can do" (Proverbs 4:7 GNT). I love this statement. Once you really believe it, you'll give your time and energy to acquiring wisdom. But the great truth of Proverbs 9:11–12 is this: Once you obtain wisdom, *you are the one who benefits*!

The wisdom of God that I write about in this book took years of seeking, searching, and listening—coupled with both positive and negative experiences. But as you'll discover, it's not only me, but others that I've had the privilege to interview who've walked wisely and borne tremendous fruit. I can only hope that, in a short amount of time, you will receive what took me years to obtain, and that you will go much farther with this wisdom than I have. It's a kingdom matter—we are all one, so if you benefit, then I benefit. If you go farther than me, it's also to my advantage, because we are one. We are all working for a common purpose and for the glory of one King.

A HIDDEN SECRET

Let's transition into the next chapter with this question: Would you be interested in knowing a hidden secret that most people are unaware of, that will propel your abilities beyond what you've ever experienced?

I think so! And here's the thing—there is such a secret. It's a hidden truth that we are about to uncover.

REFLECT

1. According to Ephesians 2:10, God planned things for you to do before you were born. Have you sought to know these plans? What has hindered your discovery of them?

2. You were born on purpose for a purpose. In light of Stan's story, how do you view your gifts and abilities? Do you view them as important for building God's kingdom? Or have you, like Stan, failed to connect the dots?

3. Doing the will of God strengthens us. Is what you're doing with your life strengthening you? Are you passionate about the work you're doing? If not, why do you lack fulfillment?

Having then gifts differing according to the grace that is given to us, let us use them.

—Romans 12:6 NKJV

2

Imparted Abilities

I have a friend, Jim, who had coached a high school girls' basket-ball team for eighteen years. In all that time, they were not able to win the state championship. Year after year, the team was either beaten in the regional finals or, if they made it to the state tourna-ment, eliminated before the final round.

Jim shared with me, "I was frustrated and ready to quit, but around that time period, I discovered the power of God's grace."

Jim made a firm decision. He would no longer coach in his own strength, as he had done for eighteen years, but would completely rely on *the grace of God*. He asked the Lord what to do, and God's response was, "Restructure your practices. Instead of ninety minutes on the floor, spend forty-five minutes in the locker room reading the Bible, sharing, and praying, and then spend the last forty-five minutes on the floor."

Jim told me, "John, this seemed counterproductive. We needed to work on skills and run plays; I needed every bit of the ninety minutes for practice. But I knew I'd heard from God."

Continuing his story, "I then gave the new strategy to the girls. They thought it was a bit religious and seemed like a silly idea. Some were even frustrated when they first heard it, but after further sharing my heart, they bought in."

With a smile on his face, he said, "That year we won the state basketball championship for the first time. If that wasn't enough, the next year we won it again."

He further commented on the second state championship, "It was mind-blowing, as we missed every layup in the final game. We should never have won with all those missed shots! However, after reviewing the stats, we realized we set a record in that game for three-point baskets. The three-pointers compensated for all the missed layups and gave us the score we needed to win."

EMPOWERMENT

Jim tapped into divine wisdom; in fact, it was the same insight the apostle Paul discovered—one that statistically eludes over ninety percent of the twenty-first-century church. The insight is this: Biblical *grace* is not only God's gift of salvation, but His *empowerment* for our lives. Examine Paul's words, but keep in mind, these words are an exact quote from the mouth of God: "*My grace* is all you need, for *My power* is greatest when you are *weak*" (2 Corinthians 12:9 GNT).

There's no question or gray area here. God directly refers to *His grace* as being *His empowerment*. The word *weak* in the above verse means "inability." The Lord declares to Paul, and also to you and me, "My empowerment (grace) is optimized in situations that are beyond your natural ability."

Eighteen years of Jim's hard work, trying with all he had to lead his girls into a championship, and what did it yield? Nothing other than years of falling short. But it was well worth the agony and multiple disappointments for the wisdom Jim would finally discover: *God's grace empowers us to go beyond our natural ability.*

In a different letter, Paul makes a rather bold statement: "I have worked harder than any of the other apostles." Wow, did he really write this? Think of who's included in this list: Peter, James, John, Barnabas, Apollos, and a slew of other great ones. Sounds a little arrogant, but if you read the rest of his statement, you realize it isn't:

> I have worked harder than any of the other apostles, although it
> was not really my own doing, but God's grace working with me.
> (1 Corinthians 15:10 GNT)

Paul is boasting of God's empowerment, not his own ability, so there's no personal bragging involved. He relied on grace to accomplish his divine mission. After years of frustration and eventual enlightenment as a coach, Jim now depends on God's empowerment (grace) to go further than his own ability. He's carried this wisdom into all aspects of his life; his ax has been sharpened!

With this in mind, let's return to our individual mission. Again, God's Word declares, "For we are His workmanship, created in Christ Jesus for good works, which God prepared beforehand that we should walk in them" (Ephesians 2:10 NKJV). God Himself prepared your assignment, even before your birth. This crafted calling is what will bring you true fulfillment; no other work or play will! It's your purpose and is remarkable in magnitude. In fact, in regard to accomplishing it, there's a critical truth to know:

> *Your destiny, which God prepared for*
> *you, is beyond your natural ability!*

Let me make this abundantly clear. It is utterly impossible for us to fulfill our divine assignment in our own ability. How do I know this to be true? Because God firmly declares that *He will share His glory with no one* (see Isaiah 48:11 NKJV). If any of us were to accomplish our divine destiny in our own ability, then God would have to share His glory with us, and He will not do this! God intentionally made your calling beyond your natural ability so you would have to depend on His *grace* to fulfill it!

SPECIFIC ABILITIES

Next, we should ask whether there are specific endowments of grace. In other words, in the same way that grace empowers us to live beyond our natural ability, are there unique capabilities we receive from God to equip us to accomplish our specific mission?

Allow me to answer with several examples. Roger Federer could never have become one of the world's greatest tennis players if he had no access to a tennis racquet and balls. The finest woodworking craftsman in the city would never have been discovered if he had no tools. You would never have known who Michelangelo was if he never had access to a chisel, brush, or paint. Is the same true for our divine callings?

Two quick stories will help clarify. When I first started in ministry, I met an exceptional praise and worship leader. This gentleman led worship for a world-renowned evangelist in the mid-1900s. The evangelist passed away in the 1970s, and this worship leader branched out into his own ministry.

He frequented our church in the 1980s, and I often found myself just staring and listening with awe—he was very gifted! He could play the piano like few I'd heard, and with no apparent effort. In no time flat, he could motivate thirty-five hundred people to stand on their feet, singing and dancing. When he praised God, the entire atmosphere changed; it was charged with God's presence.

The last few times he came to minister, I had the privilege of hosting him. Having this time together, I asked questions because I wanted to know about his God-given abilities. I discovered that his mother, a godly and devout woman, prayed many hours a day. He said, "John, when I was in my mother's womb, a man (his mother believed it was an angel) came to the house one day. This man, who my mother had never seen before, said, 'Your son will lead multitudes into the presence of God and will play the piano skillfully at a young age.'"

Then came the part of his story that astounded me, making it unforgettable. As a toddler, one day he sat down at his parents' piano and began to play perfectly, without any previous lessons or practice. It wasn't "Chopsticks," but rather a complex piece that only experienced piano students would tackle. And, of course, he did it without any sheet music.

From that day forward, he played skillfully, not once reading a note of music; he played every song by ear. He had the ability to hear a song and play it within moments.

His ministry began as a young boy playing in the main services of his hometown church. Eventually, his gift opened the door to play for the famous evangelist.

It's obvious he had a gift—a divine ability.

Another well-known gifted person, Akiane Kramarik, without any art lessons, started drawing exceptionally at the age of four. At the age of six, she advanced to painting complex objects as well as her unique visions. At the age of eight she painted the now-famous *Prince of Peace,* a portrait that hangs behind my desk.

It's obvious, she has a gift—a divine ability.

Why do only some get gifts? Or is this actually the case?

The question we should ask is: Do some, or many, or even all of God's children receive gifts? Let's look again at this chapter's opening verse of Scripture from the New Living Translation:

In His *grace,* God has given us different *gifts* for doing certain things well. (Romans 12:6)

We see two very important, but distinct, words in this one verse of scripture. The first, we've already discussed—*grace* is the Greek word *charis*. Let's add a *ma* onto *charis* and we come up with another Greek word, *charisma*; it's the word for *gifts* in the previously mentioned verse and will be our focus.

In the years of studying Greek dictionaries and examining the context of how *charisma* is used in the New Testament, I've come up with a definition:

> *Charisma:* A specific endowment of grace that empowers an individual with a special ability.

This ability is actually a divine capability that God entrusts to an individual, and it always exceeds mainstream natural ability. Some gifts are clearly supernatural. On the other hand, others seem like natural human abilities, but in reality, are extraordinary. Some gifts were given at birth, and others are given at a specific time by the Word of the Lord.

WRITING *CHARISMA*

Let me begin our exploration of *charisma* by using my life as an example. (I've written briefly about these personal stories in a previous book, *Driven by Eternity*.)

A *charisma* on my life is writing. Unless you've followed our ministry for years, you probably don't know that English, creative writing, and foreign language were my very worst subjects in school. I sometimes think my English teachers passed me just so they wouldn't have to endure another year with me!

When our class was given a writing assignment of merely a page or two, it would take me hours to accomplish what should have been a quick task. I would write a sentence or two, stare at it for a few minutes, and with every passing moment, grow more and more disgusted by how choppy and pathetic it sounded. Eventually, I'd crumple up the paper only to start the process again. I would repeat this over and over, wasting a lot of good paper, time, and mental energy. I recall occasions in which I had been writing for an hour and still didn't have the first two paragraphs completed.

If you doubt my personal assessment, then let me cite my SAT score. As you likely know, the SAT is a required examination prior to entering many colleges or universities. Back when I took the test, there were two major areas covered, *mathematics* and *verbal*. The *verbal* was, in essence, an English exam. It tested reading and writing abilities. The highest you could score was 800 points. My score for the *verbal* was 370 (yes, you read that correctly). If you look at the percentage, it was a whopping 42 percent—that is an F on most grade curves. In all my travels during the past thirty-plus years, I've only met one individual who scored lower than I on the *verbal* SAT score.

Now let's fast-forward to my early thirties. One summer morning in 1991, while I was out praying in a remote, deserted place, God spoke to me: "Son, I want you to write."

I laughed within myself, "God, You must have so many of us sons and daughters on this earth that You are getting us confused with one another. You don't want me to write; just ask my English teachers from high school."

There was no response. Just silence.

I took His silence as agreement. I convinced myself I got out of it, because there wasn't a retort from Him. But my heart knew better.

Ten months later, two different women came to me from two different states, within two weeks of each other, and spoke the exact same words: "John Bevere, if you don't write what God is giving you to write, He will give the messages to someone else, and one day you will have to give an account for it."

When the second woman from Texas spoke the exact words that the first woman from Florida had spoken, the holy fear of God came on me, and I acted. It was 1992 and there were no iPads, just pen and paper, so I took a sheet of notebook paper and wrote in bold letters on the top, *CONTRACT*. I then scribed:

> *Father, I can't write. So in order to obey You, I need grace! If I do write, then my request is that every word would be inspired by Your Spirit and it would be flooded with Your anointing. I ask that it would change men, women, children, churches, cities, and nations. I vow in advance to give You all the honor, praise, glory, and thanksgiving. I seal this contract (covenant) with You in Jesus's mighty name.*
>
> *Your son and servant, John Bevere*

Let's fast-forward to today, almost thirty years later. Currently, I've written over twenty books and they number in the tens of millions. Many of them have been on several best-selling lists in both general and Christian markets, both nationally and internationally. The books are in over one hundred languages all over the world, and in several nations are the most published books both in secular and Christian categories.

In almost every book, I had not *heard*, *read*, or *thought of* twenty to thirty percent of the written content. It came to me while typing on the keyboard. I recall several times being in either my home office or hotel room and becoming overwhelmed by what was being typed out. A few of those times I've jumped up shouting, "Wow, that is so good!"

You may ask, How could you say that? That's prideful.

To this I answer, I know where this content came from—*not me*. I fully believe my name is on these books because I was the first person outside of heaven to get to read them! I know the words came from the Holy Spirit. It's not unlike the apostle Paul who also sounded a little arrogant when he penned the words, "I have worked harder than any of the other apostles." Doesn't that sound a bit like someone who is competitive, egotistical, and even narcissistic? However, we know from Scripture that Paul was bragging on God's gift of grace rather than his own ability.

I personally believe that when God spoke to me in prayer that summer morning, the *charisma* to write was *released* into my life. But it wasn't until I made the decision to obey God that it was *activated* in my life. There are some who would argue this point, and permit me to say up front, it's not important enough to debate. I realize I could be wrong in my belief, so let me give voice to what others would counter.

Some would contend that the gift was given the moment I was born again in 1979. I can't address this discussion by experience because I didn't try writing anything between 1979 and 1992, when I wrote the contract. One thing I can say for certain: I wasn't born with this gift like the pianist I described earlier in this chapter. This does, however, settle the main point that some gifts are given right from conception. For example, we know from Scripture that John the Baptist was filled with the Spirit of God (who gives gifts) right from his mother's womb, because he recognized the living Christ in Mary's womb when he was still in his mother Elizabeth's womb (see Luke 1:41). Thirty years later, it was this same gift in John that was able to recognize Jesus (before anyone else) when He came to be baptized (see John 1:29).

On the other hand, some gifts come later. Saul, son of Kish, was a man who did not begin his life prophesying. This didn't happen until he was a young man and Samuel anointed him with oil to be the first king of Israel. Samuel stated that Saul would later see a group of men who would be playing instruments and prophesying. To quote Samuel directly, "At that time the Spirit of the LORD will come powerfully upon you, and you will prophesy with them. You will be changed into a different person" (1 Samuel 10:6).

In looking at these two different testimonies from Scripture, we clearly see how some gifts are given right from a mother's womb and others are given later.

SPEAKING *CHARISMA*

Another *charisma* on my life is public speaking. Sharing about this gift will strengthen our understanding.

The first time my wife, Lisa, heard me speak the Word of God in a service setting was memorable. To put it mildly, it was a colossal failure, and I'm not exaggerating. She fell sound asleep within the first five minutes of my message and continued in and out of sleep the entire time. It was an awful message. In fact, her best friend, Amy, sitting next to her, fell into such a deep sleep that I saw saliva drooling out of her wide-open mouth while she was in la-la land! Honestly, I was a pathetic public communicator.

At that time I was serving in my local church as an assistant to my pastor and his wife. (Our church was very influential in the United States, with over four hundred paid staff members.) My post was to take care of my pastor's family's needs and all guest ministers who came to our church. No gray area here; my kingdom responsibility was not the oracle gift, rather to serve behind the scenes. (I'll speak of this in a later chapter.)

Yet I was trying to start my own ministry because God had shown me that I would proclaim His Word to the nations of the world. My error then: I was doing it in my own strength. And I was also still in the season of primarily serving another person's ministry—being "faithful [to] what is another man's" (see Luke 16:12 NKJV). I did use all of my free time and energy to produce, package, and market my messages. (It would have been so much better if I'd focused on being a better servant and husband to my wife during that time, but we sometimes have to learn from the school of hard knocks.)

In short, I was birthing an "Ishmael ministry." Why do I call it this? There is a parallel in Scripture. God spoke to Abram (Abraham) at seventy-five years of age that he would be father to a promised son and through him eventually become the father of many nations. Ten years after the promise was made, there was still no baby, and he was now eighty-five years old. So Abraham and his wife, Sarai, devised a plan to "help" God bring to pass what He'd promised. From this vain human effort Ishmael was born. Hence, I identify this type of endeavor as an Ishmael ministry.

It's hard to believe, but some people actually gave me money. I sold them on my self-appointed mission, "Bevere Ministries." Our tagline was "Reaching the World through His Marvelous Light." I'm laughing at my stupidity and immaturity as I'm typing this. Our Ishmael's first four-part cassette tape series actually contained the message that put my wife and her best friend to sleep! How many others were lulled to sleep and drooled listening to that tape series? I shudder thinking about it!

Believe it or not, the story gets worse. During this time my hero was a great evangelist, T.L. Osborn, who is now in heaven. He and his wife led over fifty million people into salvation in their lifetime. I wanted to pattern my preaching after him. I would listen to his messages for hours on end, learning his voice pitch, inflections, teachings,

power statements, and even his humor. I wasn't just an original bor-
ing preacher but an awful copy of someone else.

T.L. was a master communicator. When he spoke at our church,
everyone listened intently to every word. Once he was telling of a
great move of God in one of their massive crusades in Africa. While
sharing with us, he was so overwhelmed by the notable miracles that
he excitedly exclaimed, "Wow!" Then he paused—we were all on the
edge of our seats—and in jest he then blurted out, "That word is so
amazing that it's the same backward: Wow!" Everyone laughed; it
came out in a way that only he could do it.

Being silly and naive, I picked that one up and started saying
"wow" regularly. I did it the same way T.L. had done in that one
unique incident. The only problem—no one ever laughed, but of
course, I didn't get it.

After falling flat on my face time and time again in my personal
strivings, I eventually broke. But then an amazing change happened. I
once again started to enjoy my current position of serving. I now gave
my free time to my marriage and friends. Life was full, rich, and complete now that the striving was past. Once I found true contentment,
it was easy to see that all my efforts were futile, making it easy to scrap
"Bevere Ministries." I knew that God would bring forth one day what
He'd promised, but it wouldn't happen by my initiation.

Once I got to this place of peace and serenity, you guessed it; God's
promotion came within months. I was asked to be the youth pastor of
one of the fastest-growing churches in the United States.

I will never forget the first Sunday. Our church's pastor was world
renowned. During this time, people would line up every Sunday for
over an hour in the hot sun to get a good seat in our auditorium,
which was packed every service. There were always visitors from
other states and nations attending our services.

The service was in full swing. We'd had a magnificent time of worship. One of the first things our pastor did when taking the platform was to inform the church of the new youth pastor—me. He then, to my surprise, asked me to come up and address the Sunday morning crowd for a couple of minutes.

Unbeknownst to me, at that moment, my wife panicked. I probably would have, too, if I would have had time to think about it. *Shock!* I'd been asked to address twenty-eight hundred people. Lisa dreaded the outcome as, from past experiences, she knew what was coming. How could we recover from this looming disaster? It would probably be the last time most in the sanctuary would hear me, because it was certain that, after this, I wouldn't be asked to speak to the main service again. All these fears mounted in her as I walked up to the platform. She told me afterward that she anxiously prayed that I wouldn't do my T.L. Osborn imitation, especially my "default awkward moment" routine of saying "wow" backward!

Once I was on the platform, our senior pastor turned over the microphone. Within sixty seconds, the entire church was on their feet cheering, applauding, and shouting in excitement about what I was saying. I spoke for four to five minutes, with the twenty-eight hundred people on their feet the entire time. I then handed the microphone back to my pastor and returned to my seat. I shook for the next five minutes from the adrenaline, or the presence of God, or probably both.

My wife was stunned, in disbelief of what had just happened. She told me after the service, "John, I thought, *who just inhabited my husband's body?*"

We had lived in Texas during my first ministry position, but this new church was in Florida. For years, the way she described it to those who asked: "John turned into another man the moment we crossed the Florida line." It was a similar statement made regarding Saul once the gift of God came on his life (see 1 Samuel 10:6).

Ever since that time, I've been preaching, teaching, and speaking before audiences and most of the time have done so with ease (I'll explain the difficult times in a later chapter). It's no longer a labor to do so. It comes without the striving I experienced in my Ishmael days. The different results between the Ishmael and Isaac times were as vast as night and day.

Let's fast-forward eight to ten years from that first Sunday in Florida. By this time, Messenger International was well established. We were doing some spring cleaning in our garage. While going through boxes and tubs, we came upon the original masters of that tape series, including the one I'd lulled Lisa and her friend to sleep with. Without hesitating, I turned to throw it in the garbage bin. All of a sudden, I heard the Holy Spirit address me: "Son, do not throw away that master tape."

I quickly countered, "Why not? It's awful; no one should ever have to listen to that message again. It should be destroyed."

Again, I heard, "Don't do it."

Knowing full well I'd heard from God, I retorted, "Why?"

"It is protection for you," the Lord said so clearly in my heart.

"Protection?"

Then came the wisdom: "Son, I always want you to know how terrible a communicator you are without Me."

With each passing year, I recognize more fully the "protection" factor. In the past three decades, the gift has operated powerfully, producing an abundance of fruit. In countless incidents, I've witnessed atmospheres shift, eruptions of praise to revelations, countless lives saved, and the manifestation of numerous miracles. Many have commented on how their lives or churches have permanently changed. With all of this fruit, it would have been easy to think I had something to do with it, but I can honestly say with the apostle Paul, "Yet it was not I but God who was working through me by His grace" (1 Corinthians 15:10). In all these years, I haven't forgotten how awful I was without God's *charisma*.

ARE YOU GIFTED?

These are two of the God-given gifts that are on my life to serve and build others. Can you relate to the struggles I experienced? Perhaps they make your own struggles in locating the *charisma* on your life seem more normal. Or, maybe as you read these accounts, your frustration has grown as you are thinking, *I don't have any gifts*. I assure you that you do, and it will become clear in the next two chapters.

I did promise to answer the question; Do some, or many, or even all of God's children receive gifts? The immediate answer is yes! And I will prove this from Scripture shortly. Not only will this question be thoroughly covered, but before the end of this book, you'll have a firm grasp on how to locate your *charisma*, develop and operate in it, and thus multiply your effectiveness in building God's kingdom.

REFLECT

1. Biblical grace is not only God's gift of salvation, but His empowerment for our lives. How have you viewed God's grace? After reading this chapter, how has your understanding of grace changed?

2. Your destiny, which God prepared for you, is beyond your natural ability. Why did God design it this way? How can you access God's empowering grace that's available to you in abundance?

3. Do some, many, or even all of God's children receive gifts? What gifts and abilities have you received? How do you see these gifts as beneficial to others?

Be honest in your evaluation of yourselves.

—Romans 12:3

3

Assess Yourself Honestly

Now that I've shared the struggle of having to both identify and walk in the *charisma* on my life, I want to briefly share what I'm *not* gifted at.

It'd be impossible to make an exhaustive list—there are just too many. First on the list is singing and playing musical instruments. Anytime I sing at home, my wife and children politely, but firmly, ask me to sing to myself.

During high school athletics, while in the gym locker room showers, I sang only once. The reaction was intense; a handful of guys in unison shouted at me to zip it, and one guy, in jest, threw a shampoo bottle my way.

My parents gave all of us Bevere children piano lessons. My teacher was a professional pianist, quite renowned in our hometown. She had made a career of teaching piano and was good at it. But after four hard years of lessons, she approached my parents and pleaded with them to allow me to quit. I was that bad!

As time passed, I thought it was just the piano, so a few years later I tried a different instrument. After we bought a classical guitar, we found a well-known teacher. He was patient and worked meticulously with me; I gave it my full effort, practiced diligently, but I struggled. It was another year and a half of lessons before I could admit that I just didn't have musical ability.

What's the long-term outcome? Let's just say that nothing has happened through the years. It's completely different than the story of my writing. At no time has any musical ability suddenly manifested in my life.

SELF-EVALUATION

I could carry on listing the things I'm not gifted at, but you get the point. It's safe to say, we all tend to know what we don't do well. Sometimes I wish it were as easy to identify our gifts as it is to pinpoint what we're not gifted at.

With that in mind, let's move on to more of Paul's instructions:

> Because of the privilege and authority God has given me, I give
> each of you this *warning*: Don't think you are better than you
> really are. Be honest in your evaluation of yourselves, measur-
> ing yourselves by the faith God has given us. Just as our bodies
> have many parts and each part has a special function, so it is
> with Christ's body. We are many parts of one body, and we all
> belong to each other. In His grace, God has given us different
> gifts for doing certain things well. (Romans 12:3–6)

Paul begins by positioning what he's about to write as a *warning*. Let me isolate and emphasize his warning: "Don't think you are better than you really are. Be honest in your evaluation of yourselves." Here we are told to do an honest self-evaluation. Of what? Of the gifts God has placed on our lives in *real time*.

Why do I use the words *real time*? Simple. Think of the biblical example used earlier. Saul's honest assessment before he met Samuel would have been, "I cannot prophesy." This would have been true and accurate for that time. However, after he met Samuel and the gift of God came on his life, his honest assessment would have changed to, "I can prophesy."

Oh, how I wish I would have read this verse more closely when I was trying to birth my Ishmael ministry. If I had been honest, I would have realized *at the time* that I was out of my element in public speaking; however, I was gifted to serve my pastor. In my natural ability, though, I was trying to bring forth what was clearly spoken to me, revealed in prayer, and prophesied by leaders of *what would come*. It wasn't *real time* yet, and it was obvious, if I just would have heeded this command in Scripture and done an honest assessment, that I wasn't ready, I would have saved a lot of time, resources, and energy. I also would have been more effective in what I was gifted to do in *that time period*.

In regard to different gifts, Paul's words are crystal clear: "Just as our bodies have many parts and each part has a special function, so it is with Christ's body" (Romans 12:4). It's simple but quite revealing, when you consider your own body. Think about it; our fingers can do things our nose cannot do. Our nose can do things our ears cannot do. Our ears can do things our stomach cannot do. Our stomach can do things our liver cannot do, and the list goes on. So, here's the main point:

> *Happy and blessed is the person who knows*
> *their gifts and operates in them.*
> *Miserable and stressed is the person who*
> *tries to operate in someone else's gifts.*

Wouldn't it be strange if one morning you woke up and your thumb said, "I've had it! Mouth, you have been speaking for years. I'm going to do the talking today." That's ridiculous; the thumb doesn't have the capability to produce sound the way the mouth can. However, the thumb does have unique abilities that the mouth doesn't have. Suppose the mouth were to say, "I want to type on the computer today!" Again, ridiculous.

The next important question is: Why do we put such a premium on the "platform gifts"? Why is it that we view ministers who speak and worship leaders who lead congregations as possessing the ultimate gifts? Paul's words to the Corinthian church on this subject state, "Some parts of the body that seem weakest and least important are actually the most necessary" (1 Corinthians 12:22).

Let me give a practical example. Have you ever noticed that legs get attention? People make statements such as, "She's got a great set of legs," or, "Wow, his legs are muscular!"

I recall my dad—who was very conservative, disciplined, and quiet—doing something completely out of character when I was a teenager. He practically never called attention to himself. But one day he blurted out, "Son, you have a good-looking set of legs."

Shocked, I just stared at him with no response and a curious smile, wondering where he was going with this. He continued, "Do you want to know why? It's because I've got a good set of legs; you inherited them from me."

I didn't know whether to fall over laughing or to acknowledge his statement, because I was so caught off guard by this atypical behavior. I just laughed and said, "Thanks, Dad, for giving me a good set of legs."

It's true—legs get attention. But have you considered the fact that people can live without legs? I know a man who lost one leg in a car accident, but he still functions and lives a normal life.

But the liver is a different story. No one can live without a liver. It is extremely important, much more so than a leg. However, have you ever heard anyone say, "Wow, that's a remarkable liver you have. It's gorgeous!"? This will not happen!

So, listen to Paul's words again: "Some parts of the body that seem weakest and least important are actually the most necessary."

Again I ask, Why do we put such a premium on the platform gifts? They are the "seen" parts and necessary, but according to the Word of God, they are not the most important.

My friend Stan (from the first chapter) has a gift of reaching people in the business world, as well as making and giving finances. His gift seems less valuable than a platform gift, and with our established church culture, it's nonverbally communicated this way. What's been the typical underlying message in the church? "Those on the platform are the chosen ones who really have a calling on their life."

Think about it. If someone says, "He or she has a calling on his or her life," everyone immediately assumes it is the call of a pastor, worship leader, youth leader, Christian author, missionary, and so forth. Upon hearing this statement, very few would think, "He's called to the medical field and is discovering new ways to cure cancer." Or, "She's in government establishing laws to protect the advancement of the kingdom." Or, "He's in education seeding the young minds with the knowledge and wisdom of God." Or, "She's called to the marketplace to reach the lost there and to finance the building of the kingdom."

The consequences of this mindset on gifts are evident: Stan had been in church for years without the realization that he's just as "called" as I am. His God-given abilities, though valid, didn't seem as important because of this unspoken understanding that "church-related" gifts are more important than others. This needs to change! We are all called and carry the unique gifts needed to fulfill our kingdom assignment.

Here's the entirety of what Paul said to the Corinthian church:

Our bodies have many parts, and God has put each part just
where He wants it. How strange a body would be if it had only

one part! Yes, there are many parts, but only one body. The eye can never say to the hand, "I don't need you." The head can't say to the feet, "I don't need you." In fact, some parts of the body that seem weakest and least important are actually the most necessary. And the parts we regard as less honorable are those we clothe with the greatest care. So we carefully protect those parts that should not be seen, while the more honorable parts do not require this special care. So God has put the body together such that extra honor and care are given to those parts that have less dignity. This makes for harmony among the members, so that all the members care for each other. (1 Corinthians 12:18–25)

Maybe the reason we honor church-related gifts more than others is that we limit Paul's discussion to church or conference settings. It's obvious that preaching or teaching gifts are more in demand in this atmosphere. But kingdom work happens everywhere, so this is another paradigm that must see a radical shift. The Greek word for "church" is *ekklēsías*, which means, "called out." The Greek dictionary definition adds, "the called people, or those called out or assembled in the public affairs of a free state, the body of free citizens called together by a herald."[1]

Are we only the church when we are gathered within a building? Are we only a church when we get together to pray, worship, preach, or minister? This paradigm causes people to act one way in this type of setting and revert to a different behavior when in society. We are the church and are equipped with giftings to build the kingdom wherever we are 24 hours a day, 7 days a week, 365 days a year!

Recently, I met with a multibillionaire. He was conducting what he called his "God tour." He and his team had flown to various cities and attended churches and conferences to meet with certain ministers. His goal: He wanted the fivefold ministry to sharpen and further equip him for his work. My meeting with him was set up in advance by a good friend. It occurred during a conference I was speaking at in Dallas. As it turned out, we had a great three-hour lunch, and I came away feeling as if I got more out of the lunch than he did.

He shared that he had floundered in the business world early in his career, but the day came that his eyes were opened. The enlightenment began when he questioned why kingdom activity only happens in church or conference settings—why not everywhere? He knew he was called to the marketplace, but why was he conducting himself in that arena in a way that was no different than unbelievers? Nothing separated him from the world.

He determined he would "walk with God" in the marketplace and would listen to the Holy Spirit's voice, no different than a minister would on a platform. In essence, he faced off with the calling question and decided he was just as called by God as any pastor. He then identified his God-given gifts and determined to purposefully operate in them. He would listen to God's voice in his quiet times, as well as in business meetings. Sure enough, God gave him words of knowledge and wisdom for his marketplace affairs.

The results are evident; he's not floundering any longer! He shared some of the specific words from God, and they often seemed insignificant. However, he was determined to obey, even if the divine instructions went against conventional business wisdom and were uncomfortable to follow. He related the questionings, raised eyebrows, concerns, and even resistance he encountered, both with clients and his own team members. But the fruit of his steadfast confidence in the words from God proved to be worth billions. I was mesmerized by the miraculous stories he shared.

DISCIPLES OF NATIONS

If we can flip this cultural mindset about gifting in today's church, what will be the outcome? If we effectively communicated to all who hear our messages that every person is *called*, *gifted*, and *valuable* to the building of the kingdom, what would happen? It's easy; everyone would work with the purpose and passion of Billy Graham, Oral Roberts, Mother Teresa, and the apostle Paul. I observed this purpose and passion in the multibillionaire in our meeting. He knew his mission and the importance of his God-given gifts to accomplish it.

This is the paradigm we must have in order for nations to be discipled. But let's dig a little deeper into this point. Jesus doesn't say, "Make disciples of church attendees." He commands us to "Make disciples of *nations*" (see Matthew 28:19). The Greek word for "nations" is *ethnos*, which is defined as "a body of persons united by kinship, culture, and common traditions."[2] This certainly includes actual nations, tribes, territories, and ethnic groups. However, it also encompasses persons with a commonality, such as cyclists, actors, physicians, business owners, pilots, lawyers, stay-at-home moms, government workers, athletes, and many more—the list is virtually endless. We are to make disciples of the men and women in all these different circles of life.

But let's take it one step further. Jesus doesn't say, "Make disciples of the people in nations." He says, "Make disciples of nations." It's important to catch this difference; we are to shift the manner of operating in these different circles through the Word of God. Of course, this occurs first and foremost by reaching the people of these different circles. However, it goes deeper. We are to baptize (immerse) not only the people, but also their modes of operation, in the ways of the Father, Son, and Holy Spirit. An example would be assisting in transforming the thinking of those involved in the marketplace, just like the billionaire's. This is just the tip of the iceberg.

Consider Zacchaeus. He was a *chief* tax collector; no doubt one of the best in the region. In essence, he was head of the mafia in the area. He most likely was hated by the people because he did what most tax collectors did—leveraged his position for selfish gain. He probably stole from, swindled, cheated, intimidated, and dominated the citizens. He was a notorious, influential figure, so his example most likely flowed down through the ranks.

I've witnessed this in a few of the nations I've traveled to. The leader of the nation is corrupt, and he requires his officials to slip money to him under the table. Well, this behavior flows down through the ranks. Now the immigration official at the airport needs a bribe or you can't get his approval to leave the country.

Back to Zacchaeus. Jesus called him by name and, interestingly, only spoke these words to him: "Zacchaeus! . . . Quick, come down! I must be a guest in your home today."

Zacchaeus stood before the Master and responded, "I will give half my wealth to the poor, Lord, and if I have cheated people on their taxes, I will give them back four times as much!" (Luke 19:5–8)

What happened in that region in regard to tax collecting? The chief role model's mode of operations shifted from dark, worldly techniques to kingdom practices! Now this area of business/government would be conducted here on earth much more closely to the way heaven operates. A shift in society had occurred. This change didn't happen during a church service, nor did Jesus preach a message in a conference, convincing Zacchaeus to be a follower. It happened in the city center. Zacchaeus had an encounter with Jesus, and his methods of operation suddenly changed. This should happen every time people encounter us in our different nations (the circles of influence we are called to), because this same Jesus lives in us.

I'm currently coaching a former NFL football player who has a large social media audience of bodybuilders. He's instructing these bodybuilders in such a way that the kingdom of heaven's culture is flowing into this nation (*ethnos* group), whether his followers are yet committed to Jesus's lordship or not. He is speaking to these people in a way that demonstrates kingdom ways and methods.

Our gifts aren't just for the gathering of saints in a building, although this is valid and important—I certainly don't want to downplay our gatherings. The intention here is to expand our view of the operation of God's gifts. If we're called outside the church, which applies to most of us, we're called to operate supernaturally through our gifts within our circle of influence—in the midst of our *ethnos* group.

If you have separated the secular from the sacred, that mentality needs to change. When you walk into the room, no matter where it is—the hospital room for your work as a surgeon or nurse; the classroom for your work as a public school teacher; the factory as a machinist, and so forth—you've been gifted to bring the sacred into that atmosphere and to disciple it in the name of the Father, Son, and Holy Spirit. In other words, you have their backing and authority to bring heaven to earth, no differently than Jesus did with Zacchaeus and others. You are called to multiply the kingdom's mode of operation throughout your arena of influence.

Doesn't this make going to the office or school so much more of an adventure?

REFLECT

1. Scripture warns us to be honest in our evaluation of ourselves. This assessment should be done in *real time*. I shared the story of when I tried to start a ministry before its time. How can you avoid making the same mistake? What are you gifted to do at present in this season?

2. Happy and blessed is the person who knows their gifts and operates in them. Miserable and stressed is the person who tries to operate in someone else's gifts. Have you ever been tempted to pursue an area of gifting that's different than your calling? If so, why?

3. Our gifts aren't just for the gathering of saints in a building, but also for our specific areas of influence. How can you view your everyday life as vital to building God's kingdom? In what ways can you use your vocational gifts for kingdom purposes?

Let a man so consider us,
as servants of Christ and stewards
of the mysteries of God.

—1 Corinthians 4:1 NKJV

4

Stewards

We've showcased the words *grace* and *gift*; now we'll turn our focus toward *stewardship*. After we establish an understanding of this word, then we can join all three words together from Scripture to discover a clear mandate for our lives.

Merriam-Webster defines *stewardship* as "the careful and responsible management of something entrusted to one's care." It's prudent to examine Greek definitions of key words, because often the translated words don't carry the exact meaning. However, this is not the case with stewardship; the meaning in Greek and English is quite similar. The Greek word for *steward* in the above verse is *oikonomos*. It is defined as "one who has the authority and responsibility for something—one who is in charge of, one who is responsible for, administrator, manager."[3]

There are three clear aspects of stewardship derived from both definitions:

- Oversees what belongs to another.
- Carries authority to manage what has been entrusted.
- Is responsible: he or she will give an account to the owner.

God created and owns everything! Psalm 24:1 declares, "The earth *is* the LORD's, and all its fullness" (NKJV). This makes us stewards over everything in this realm. We are to manage the earth—all land, water, air, resources, animals, fish, and fowl. We are responsible to care for the good of human beings spiritually, emotionally, intellectually, and physically. This includes all godly and beneficial knowledge, wisdom, and understanding. I could continue, but in essence, we are responsible for everything on earth, both seen and unseen.

But let's drill down to the precise usage of stewardship in Paul's statement. He writes of being "stewards of the mysteries of God." The New Living Translation says we "have been *put in charge* of explaining God's mysteries." One of the gifts (*charismas*) on Paul's life was revelation; to communicate mysteries—hidden truths that had not yet been revealed. Therefore, the exact *stewardship* he refers to is not managing money, time, resources (all valid stewardships), but rather managing the gift (*charisma*) on his life. Does this also apply to us?

Peter writes: "As each one has received a *gift*, minister it to one another, as good *stewards* of the manifold *grace* of God" (1 Peter 4:10 NKJV). All our highlighted words are found in this one verse (gift: *charisma*; stewards: *oikonomos*; and grace: *charis*). Peter informs us, no differently than Paul, of our entrusted stewardship of *charisma*. Much is revealed in this one statement, so we should examine it carefully.

Notice that Peter writes "each one" has received a gift. It's important up front to point out that he didn't say "each minister," "each pastor," "each worship leader," or any other oracle ministry gift, but rather "each one." If you are born again, you have a gift or gifts that have been imparted and entrusted to you. This is the answer from Scripture to our question of two chapters ago. *You have a gift or gifts, and to reiterate, these gifts are specific endowments of grace that empower you with special abilities.*

To show the importance of your gifts, let's use Paul's attitude as a template. He regarded his stewardship seriously, in fact, quite seriously. A little later in the letter to the Corinthians, he writes:

If I preach the gospel, I have nothing to boast of, for necessity
is laid upon me; yes, *woe is me* if I do not preach the gospel!
For if I do this willingly, I have a reward; but if against my
will, I have been *entrusted with a stewardship*." (1 Corinthians
9:16–17 NKJV)

Immediately, my attention is captured by the words *woe is me*.
These are strong words, stronger than most of us comprehend. The
Greek word for *woe* is *ouaí*. It is defined as "disaster, horror."[4] Another
dictionary lists its meaning as "interjection of grief or indignation."[5]
Each occurrence of this word in the New Testament implies a very serious and terrifying judgment that awaits those it's ascribed to. When
Paul says, "Woe is me," it is akin to calling a curse upon himself. This
immediately should get our attention. It is a severe matter to neglect
our God-given gifts.

Paul knew that God had entrusted something of great value to
him. Here is the sobering truth: If he didn't administer it properly,
then others would not experience the benefit, and even suffer the loss,
of what God intended for them to receive. Paul knew the gift wasn't
given for him; it was given *to* others, *through* him. In other words,
he carried what God wanted others to have—thus, the reason for
the severity behind declaring "woe" onto himself for neglecting his
stewardship.

Let's revert to you and me. There are two interesting points to
highlight. First, Paul's gift was a "noticeable" gift. Recall, God has chosen the gifts that are not obvious to be held in greater honor than
those that are apparent. If Paul treated his noticeable gift with such
seriousness, we shouldn't devalue the gift God has placed on us, especially if it is not noticeable.

Even more important is the second takeaway: The gifts of God on
your life are not for you; they are *for* others to benefit *through* you. The

gift of writing is not for me but for you. The gift of speaking is not for me but for those I speak to. The gift of leading is not for me but for those I lead, and so forth.

WE CHOOSE HOW TO USE THE GIFT

We can use the gift on our life well, or misuse it—the choice is ours. The gift will still operate even if it is not used according to its original divine intent to build the kingdom. Adolf Hitler was a gifted leader and could have led his nation in a way that would have benefited millions of Germans, Jews, Russians, French, British, and so forth. Did he use this gift for God's glory or to benefit himself and those he favored? Did he use his gift to bring harm? Were Jews and numerous others plundered, devastated, tortured, and put to death for no godly cause? Did he misuse the gift of leadership on his life? The answers to these questions need no discussion—they are crystal clear.

Adolf Hitler's stewardship is obvious, but let me discuss two other well-known personalities who may not be as obvious. First, Whitney Houston, an artist who had one of the greatest voices I've heard in my lifetime. The touch of God was evident upon her life. When Whitney sang, all who heard her were deeply stirred. She was ethereal, seemingly angelic, and quite powerful.

A second example would be Freddie Mercury, the lead singer of the rock group Queen. He had the ability to move entire stadiums with his gifts of composing and singing. His ability was far from common and some would even argue supernatural. He could arouse a crowd to follow his lead in almost any setting. Years after his death, his songs are still sung widely.

Did either Whitney or Freddie manage their gifts well? No doubt, there are many who would argue that they did. But let's view this question through Jesus's words:

Wisdom is shown to be right by its *results*. (Matthew 11:19)

and again:

Wisdom is shown to be right by the *lives of those who follow it*. (Luke 7:35)

Let's examine the fruit of these two amazing entertainers—both in the short- and long-term results of their stewardship. Did Whitney use her gift to lead people into the presence of God? After listening to her sing, were her audiences moved toward godliness? Did her songs strengthen marriage covenants or foster discontent by creating an unrealistic romantic expectation? Did Freddie use his gift to move his audiences toward righteousness? Did he point people to honor their Creator? How did Whitney and Freddie depart this earth? Is their legacy enduring or fleeting? Will it last forever, or will it perish with this world?

Jesus encourages us to examine the outcome—I'll let you determine the results of Whitney's and Freddie's stewardship. However, the ultimate examination will come in the presence of our Creator. Each will give an account at the judgment.

I realize that if you are a fan of either Whitney or Freddie, you may be uncomfortable with this discussion. But let's ask a question that will shed more light on how their stewardship will be assessed at the judgment. Let's view their legacies from the vantage point of ten million years from now. How will Whitney and Freddie look back at how they managed their God-given gifts? Examining the eternal perspective may change your original view.

Life is all about perspective. If we view it through the lens of eighty years, we will see things one way. However, if we see it through the lens of the eternal perspective, things look different.

Consider this scenario: You are invited to have dinner at a cafeteria. You pay one price and may eat all you desire. There is a large table with nothing but delicious desserts. If you look at this table with a one-day perspective, what will you do? Most likely, you'll eat every dessert on the table. What if you look at the same table with a one-year perspective? You'd probably eat only one or maybe none of the desserts. Why? You don't want an upset stomach tomorrow morning, ten pounds of fat added to your body by next week, and compromised long-term health!

When we look at Whitney's and Freddie's fruit from the eternal perspective, the wisdom of their stewardship becomes clearer.

It's nonthreatening to speak of Adolf Hitler, or even Freddie Mercury or Whitney Houston. But here is the sobering reality: You and I will also have to give an account of our entrusted gifts when we stand before the Judge. Our gifts will be seen through the eternal, not the eighty-year perspective. Our gifts will be examined in the light of God's eternal Word that commissions us to build His kingdom. Will our legacy be enduring or will it pass away with the world's system?

A CLOSE LOOK AT MOTIVATION

Let me restate what was discussed in the first chapter. You can steward your gift at any given time in one of three ways:

- You can use it to build the kingdom.
- You can use it to benefit yourself.
- You can neglect it by not using it at all.

It is important to amplify the second point, which can be deceiving. There are many who think they are building others, even for the kingdom's sake, yet it's done with the motive of personal gain.

I unknowingly fell into this. Years ago, in the early days of ministry, I consistently spoke nice and pleasing words to everyone on our team, at church, and to anyone else in my world. I'd utter these happy and pleasant statements, even if they weren't true. Word got back to me of how kind and loving I was. These compliments certainly encouraged my behavior.

One day in prayer, God said to me, "People say you are a loving, caring, and kind person, don't they?"

I would normally take His words as an affirmation, but the way the Holy Spirit spoke, it didn't seem to be going this direction. So, I cautiously replied, "Yes, they do."

He immediately responded, "Do you know why you only speak nice things to people?"

Even more cautiously, I responded, "Why?"

"Because you fear their rejection," He said. "So, who is the focus of your love, you or them?"

Knowing my motives were completely and utterly exposed, I admitted His statement was true.

Then He said, "If you really loved people, you would tell them the truth—even at the risk of being rejected."

This correction dealt with my treatment of people. But in regard to our discussion here, I need to ask: Can we misuse the gift of God on our life in a similar way? In other words, it may appear to others that our gift is being used to build the kingdom, but in reality, is it being used for self-seeking motives? The answer can certainly be yes, and I will once again use myself as an example, and then support it with scriptural examples.

Normally, I don't get a direct word from the Lord as far as what to speak about at a conference or church service, but I always listen to my heart for the leading of the Spirit. That being said, there was one case in which I definitely had a word from the Lord before I spoke.

I was scheduled to minister at a conference in the Midwest. When I awoke in my hotel room on my scheduled day to speak, I undoubtedly heard the Holy Spirit say, "I want you to minister on *The Bait of Satan* in tonight's conference." (This is a book I wrote in 1994 about overcoming offenses and freely forgiving those who have hurt us.)

All day I wrestled with His instructions. *The Bait of Satan* message had been out for several years. It was a best-selling book, and I'd preached its message all over the country for an extended season, and a lot of people had already heard it. What made this direction from the Spirit even more difficult is that I was in the process of working on a new manuscript. When you're in the midst of months of writing, those truths are stronger and fresher in your heart. Bottom line, I really didn't want to speak the older message. But I had a direct word from the Holy Spirit.

Upon arriving at the auditorium that evening, I was informed by the conference coordinators that people had traveled long distances to hear me. I shuddered, thinking these travelers would probably hear a repeat message or there would be a good chance they'd read *The Bait of Satan.*

Upon walking into the auditorium, I noticed the atmosphere was energized. The anticipation of the people was obvious. It made obeying the instructions I received that morning even more difficult. Somehow, I just didn't want to disappoint the people. I yielded to the pressure and decided to speak the "fresh" message, and I was delighted with how it went. The preaching was strong and the people responded enthusiastically. Some even stood to their feet, affirming the strong points I was making. It looked as if I'd "gotten away with it," or perhaps I hadn't heard from God that morning. Either way, I was happy. Afterward, in the greenroom, everyone was pumped and thankful for a great message.

Typically, I leave a city with a sense of satisfaction and joy; it's almost as if God smiles inside my heart. This was definitely not the case the next morning. I woke up very heavy in heart, lacked energy, and was even fighting depression. Immediately, I knew why—I'd disobeyed God. The first thing I did that morning was to get down on my knees, repent, and ask for forgiveness. I pleaded for the blood of Jesus to cleanse me.

However, there was no relief. I carried the heaviness and sadness all day—the remaining time in the hotel, the trip to the airport, waiting at the airport for a delayed flight, and the trip to the West Coast. The sadness, heaviness, and depression were almost unbearable. Finally, when we were circling the city of San Diego, all of it lifted off me.

I questioned, "Father, I repented and asked forgiveness this morning. Why haven't You restored my joy, peace, and contentment until now?"

I heard the Lord say, "I allowed you to carry the weight of your disobedience so you could understand its severity. There was a pastor in the service last night who needed to hear the message I've entrusted to you—*The Bait of Satan*. It is a critical time in his life and ministry. You disobeyed Me and there are consequences. The weight you have felt is a warning to not let this happen again. This is a new city; now obey Me."

In reflecting on the prior evening, the people in attendance, the conference team, and the conference leader were all happy. I was invited back and even heard reports later of the results of that service. It's obvious that the gift of God worked through me that night, even though it wasn't used according to the divine intent.

Are you convinced this can really happen? Let's turn to incidents in Scripture to illustrate the misuse of a divine gift. Consider Moses. He was called to lead Israel to the Promised Land and was gifted to work renowned miracles to accomplish his mission.

On one occasion, God instructed Moses to speak to the rock and water would come out to give the people a drink. But Moses struck the rock out of anger, directly disobeying the divine instructions.

However, water still came out, in abundance, enough to give a drink to millions of people in the middle of the desert. It was another spectacular miracle for Moses's résumé! Once again, the people were in awe of their leader's gifting. However, afterward, when the "conference" was over, Moses was called to account for not handling the gift as God instructed. He was denied entrance to the Promised Land for his misuse. Sobering when you think about it.

Another example would be Balaam. He prophesied over Israel, and his words are still recorded in Scripture to this day. Wow, what a great testimony, to have your prophesy in the eternal Word of God! But there's more to the story: God specifically told him not to go—not to do what others wanted. Yet, Balaam's entrusted gift operated even when God directly commanded him, "'You shall not go with them'" (Numbers 22:12 NKJV). Once again, the gift operated outside of original divine intent.

Here is the bottom line. God is not a micromanager of His entrusted gifts. If He oversaw us in this manner, we wouldn't be called *stewards*. For a steward is given authority to manage what is entrusted to him or her without direct supervision. A scriptural example of this would be Jesus's parable of the unjust steward:

> There was a certain rich man who had a *steward*, and an
> accusation was brought to him that this man was wasting
> his goods. So he called him and said to him, "What is this
> I hear about you? Give an account of your *stewardship*, for
> you can no longer be *steward*." (Luke 16:1–2 NKJV)

Since stewardship was more common in the Bible's days than today, it's easy to miss something significant here. Notice there was a season in which the rich man was ignorant of what was transpiring. He wasn't watching the steward's movements day by day. It took a report from someone else to get his attention of the mismanagement that had been going on for a good while.

This is seen again with Joseph in the book of Genesis. In Egypt he started out as a slave in Potiphar's house, but eventually he was promoted and made a *steward* of the entire household. We read, "So Potiphar gave Joseph complete administrative responsibility over everything he owned. With Joseph there, he didn't worry about a thing—except what kind of food to eat!" (Genesis 39:6). Potiphar didn't micromanage or supervise Joseph's work. He entrusted Joseph with a stewardship.

This is similar to the gifts God places in you and me. The apostle Peter charges us to be good stewards of the manifold grace of God on our lives—the *charisma*.

UNOBVIOUS ETERNAL GIFTS

Let's drill deeper. First, let's refresh our memory of Peter's words: "As each one has received a gift, *minister* it to one another, as good stewards." As stewards we are expected to *minister*, or use the gifts. Again, they are not for us but for others. The word for *minister* is *diakonéō*, and is defined as "to serve, wait upon, with emphasis on the work to be done."[6] We must maintain a serving attitude with our gifts. Our gifts were freely given and we are to use these gifts willingly with the purpose of building other's lives.

We are to "minister *our entrusted gifts* to one another, as good stewards of the *manifold* grace of God." The word *manifold* here means "of various kinds."[7] It would take too many pages to list the various gifts God has given to His people. In fact, it's probably not possible to compile such a list. Some gifts are obvious in their connection to building the kingdom. However, many more are a challenge to identify. Here's an example.

I recently heard a well-known pastor talk about an interesting conversation that transpired just prior to his yearly conference. This annual event is popular and well-attended. As the team was setting up the auditorium, the pastor saw a medical doctor, who was a member of his church, putting handouts on the seats for the conference delegates.

The pastor went to the doctor and apologized, "Doctor, you shouldn't be doing this. We have interns and other volunteers who can handle this."

The pastor reported that the doctor sternly but politely corrected him, "I take off from my medical practice every year for this conference. It's my most treasured week of the year because I get to do something to build the kingdom of God."

In listening to my pastor friend tell this story, I grieved for this doctor. I realized he hadn't connected the dots on the value of his gift in building God's kingdom. Again, some gifts directly connect while most are indirect, but not any less important.

This doctor was no different than Stan in the first chapter. What if there were no doctors? What happens when people who are called in other areas to build the kingdom get sick or diseased? Many would be taken out early without medical help.

Let's conduct a hypothetical scenario illustrating the connection. A doctor uses his gift by assisting in restoring the health of a stay-at-home mom. As a result, since this woman is not helplessly sick in bed and eventually dying prematurely, she is able to flourish in her gift of raising her children in a godly way. One child is gifted in the area of innovation, and her mother encourages it. After the daughter graduates with a computer software degree, she takes a position working for a company that develops software.

This grown daughter, now fully operating in her gift, designs a new way of communicating that is far more effective than anything on the market. However, her innovation will not go far without her coworker in the advertising department. He uses his gift to give an awareness to retailers and consumers of the potential of this new software package.

One of the retailers, a company owned by a gifted businesswoman, picks up the product. This retail store has a sales team, and one man exercises his gift to sell the software package to a ministry that is called to disciple the nations of the world.

This ministry has a gifted IT person who recognizes the potential of this software and recommends purchasing it. He integrates the software into their existing system.

As a result, this ministry now has the capability to more effectively impact pastors and leaders globally. The results: Exponentially more men and women come to salvation and are discipled through the avenue of this software communication package.

At the judgment seat, Jesus will show the doctor, who originally treated the stay-at-home mother, the multitudes of peoples he reached in the nations of the world. We can almost imagine what will transpire. The doctor will question, "No, that can't be me. I never went to those nations."

Jesus will then show him that, because he was faithful to the gift on his life, it resulted in the chain reaction that eventually led to numerous salvations and the strengthening of believers that occurred globally. Jesus will most likely say to this doctor, "You worked willingly in your medical practice as though you were working for the Lord rather than for people, and your fruit is evident. Many were impacted due to your obedience. Well done, good and faithful servant!"

You may be questioning, *Is this idea really supported in the Bible?* Read this:

In all the work you are doing, work the best you can. Work as if
you were doing it for the Lord, not for people. Remember that you
will receive your reward from the Lord. (Colossians 3:23–24 NCV)

This is just one scenario. There are countless possibilities of these
kinds of connections or chain reactions.

Let's return to the actual story of my pastor friend. What if the
doctor gets fed up with only being fulfilled one week a year? (Of
course, the lack of satisfaction is fueled by the ignorance of his gift's
importance.) It's quite possible that eventually he'd walk away from
the medical field, seeking to be fulfilled fifty-two weeks a year. Let's
assume he accepts a position at his church teaching and developing
curriculum for discipleship classes. What would happen at the judgment seat? Would he receive as great of a reward since he had walked
away from his entrusted gift?

Sadly, I've often witnessed men and women struggle in positions
of full-time ministry because of not recognizing that their gifts would
flourish in arenas outside the church environment.

It takes knowledge, spiritual sensitivity, and maturity to see the
unobvious positions of kingdom service.

Here is the raw truth: Your gift, whether it operates best in healthcare, education, government, athletics, the marketplace, the arts, the
media, the home, or any other arena, has a connection to building the
kingdom. The Master Planner designed it this way.

It's quite possible that we may not recognize the connections of
our obedience and success until we actually stand before Jesus at the
judgment seat. As Paul writes, "It is the same way with good works,
even if they are not known at first, they will eventually be recognized
and acknowledged" (1 Timothy 5:25 TPT).

So, whether or not your gift is evident, your charge is, "As the
Lord has called each one, so let him walk" (1 Corinthians 7:17 NKJV).

MOTIVATION IS CRUCIAL

Let's return to Paul's words that we are using as a template for our stewardship:

> For necessity is laid upon me; yes, woe is me if I do not preach the gospel! For if I do this *willingly*, I have a *reward*. (1 Corinthians 9:16–17 NKJV)

The next truth to highlight is that our "reward" is directly connected to our "willingness" or, in a more general sense, our "attitude." Simply put, if our attitude is *selfless*, we receive a reward; if our attitude is *selfish*, we don't receive a reward.

The different scenarios of *selfless* or *selfish* motives are vast, too many to list. Let's highlight just a few comparisons. A selfless attitude could be: *What a privilege to serve others with my entrusted abilities.* A *selfish* motive would sound more like this: *What can I gain from my ability?* To put it more directly, the first is, *What can I do for you?* The second is, *What's in it for me?*

Another selfless attitude would be, *I'll do my very best, no matter what I get in return*, whereas the selfish motive is, *Why should I do a thorough job when there's not much in it for me?*

Still another selfless motive: *I must keep pressing on; there are so many to impact.* Whereas the selfish one would be, *I'm successful; I can take it easy now.*

Paul writes on the importance of *attitudes* or *motives*: "Let a man so consider us, as servants of Christ and *stewards*," and these words are immediately followed by:

> As for me, it matters very little how I might be evaluated by you or by any human authority. I don't even trust my own judgment

on this point. My conscience is clear, but that doesn't prove I'm right. It is the Lord Himself who will examine me and decide. So don't make judgments about anyone ahead of time—before the Lord returns. For He will bring our *darkest secrets* to light and will reveal our *private motives*. Then God will give to each one whatever *praise* is due. (1 Corinthians 4:3–5)

Paul is not concerned about the evaluation of his friends, critics, or any other self-appointed authority—not even his own opinion. These assessments are meaningless compared to what all of us will eventually face—the divine examination. What matters is how *Jesus* will evaluate stewardship.

To be sure, our obedient *actions* or *works* will certainly be important at the judgment. Jesus clearly states, "Look, I am coming soon, bringing My reward with Me to repay all people according to their deeds" (Revelation 22:12). It is not an "either/or" scenario but rather a "both/and" scenario—*both motives* and *works* will be examined at the judgment.

Some may think Paul is referencing the unbeliever's judgment—the "great white throne judgment"—where unbelievers will give an account for their sins due to not receiving the saving grace of Jesus Christ. This is definitely not the case, because at the great white throne judgment no one will receive "praise" from God, as stated by Paul.

It's important to maintain the context of his subject matter; Paul is discussing *stewardship*. There's no doubt as to what he's referencing. Our "darkest secrets" and "private motives" in handling our gifts will be revealed at the judgment. This really gets my attention!

Let me make it crystal clear by using my previous story of disobeying the Lord on what I should preach. Those who attended that meeting most likely to this day believe I was obedient to God in speaking my "fresh" message. I wasn't. It is quite possible that at the judgment, they will learn of my disobedience, for Jesus states:

> "The time is coming when everything that is covered up will
> be revealed, and all that is secret will be made known to all.
> Whatever you have said in the dark [our private motives and
> secrets] will be heard in the light, and what you have whispered
> behind closed doors will be shouted from the housetops for all
> to hear!" (Luke 12:2–3, bracketed clarification is mine)

It's quite possible at the judgment seat that I may be called upon to apologize to the pastor and others who didn't receive *The Bait of Satan* message that evening.

WHAT IS EXPECTED?

We've firmly established the importance of understanding stewardship. The most significant question now is: What is expected of us? In other words, What are the results Jesus will look for at the judgment when He examines how we handled His entrusted gifts? Can we know? Absolutely yes, for Jesus declares we "will be judged on the day of judgment by the truth I have spoken" (John 12:48).

We will begin this revealing and empowering discussion in the next chapter. It's the focus of this book.

REFLECT

1. Before reading this chapter, did you see yourself as a steward? Why or why not?

2. The gifts you've been given are not for you; they're to be given to others through you. In other words, you carry what God wants others to have. With this in mind, why is it important to steward your gifts faithfully? What's at stake if you neglect your stewardship?

3. At any given time, you can choose to use the gifts God has given you in one of three ways. You can use them to build the kingdom. You can use them to benefit yourself. Or you can neglect them—not using them at all. How are you using your gifts? What changes should you make regarding the way you steward what God's given to you?

Let a man so consider us, as servants of Christ and stewards of the mysteries of God. Moreover it is required in stewards that one be found faithful.

—1 Corinthians 4:1–2 NKJV

5

Faithful

The apostle Paul identifies Apollos and himself as *servants* of Jesus Christ and *stewards* of their entrusted gifts. In the previous chapter, we learned that this identity doesn't solely apply to these two great saints or only to a current church leader, but to every believer. You and I are also servants of Jesus Christ, and a primary way we fulfill this role is to be good stewards of our entrusted gifts.

Now we'll turn our attention to what's required of a steward, and there's only one attribute listed: *faithfulness*. Before diving in, let's ponder the fact that there aren't two, three, or more characteristics listed. Paul could have stated that it is required in stewards that they exude joy, or are strong, or are scholars of the Scripture, or are compassionate, or have any other godly trait. I'm not taking away from the importance of all these attributes, of course. However, I am pointing out that there's only one listed, and it is *required*. So, it's very important to home in on this virtue if we are going to be good stewards and to one day hear our Master say, "Well done."

THE DEFINITION OF FAITHFULNESS

I've had the privilege of addressing leadership teams all over the world—not just those in ministry, although ministry would be the majority—but also people on corporate, government, business, education, and athletic teams. I've asked several times for team members to give a one-word definition of *faithfulness*. Being leaders, they are usually eager to speak up. After hearing similar answers in almost every setting, I decided to make a list of the most popular responses:

- Steadfast
- Consistent
- Dependable
- Reliable
- Loyal
- True
- Trustworthy
- Devoted
- Truthful
- Resolute
- Obedient

There have been others, but these have been the most popular. Even more important, all these answers are in line with dictionary definitions and synonyms.

There is one very important definition, though, that I haven't heard—not once in any setting: "multiplication."

You may immediately think, *Multiplication? That's not a definition of faithful!* You also may be questioning my verbal skills, as did my former English teachers. However, I assure you that by the end of this chapter, you will not only agree, but most likely see it as one of the most important definitions of faithfulness.

THE PARABLE OF THE TALENTS

To introduce multiplication, let's go to Jesus's parable of the talents. Please read it carefully, even if you've read it numerous times before.

The Kingdom of Heaven can be illustrated by the story of a
man going on a long trip. He called together his servants and
entrusted his money to them while he was gone. (Matthew
25:14)

First of all, this is a parable; therefore, it's symbolic, not literal.
Thus, we need to interpret it in the light of biblical understanding—
the overall counsel of God's Word. The man going on the long trip
represents Jesus. A steward is committed to each of his servants—
they are symbolic of you and me.

Next, notice the trip is long, supporting two facts. First, it has
been almost two thousand years since Jesus left us in charge of building what He died for—the kingdom. Obviously, He hasn't returned
yet, but even at this point in history it's been a long time.

Third, this parable once again shows that stewardship is not mi-
cromanaged. The man in the parable is going away and isn't returning
every month to check up on his stewards' progress. According to the
parable, he doesn't inspect their work until he returns.

Let's continue his story:

He gave five bags of silver to one, two bags of silver to another,
and one bag of silver to the last—dividing it in proportion to
their abilities. He then left on his trip. (Matthew 25:15)

In this story, the entrustment is money. Most Bible translations
use the word *talent,* and this word is actually the most accurate, for the
Greek word is *tálanton.* A talent is a measure of weight and is mostly
used for gold or silver. One talent is roughly seventy-five pounds.
Most experts estimate one talent of silver to be worth roughly $18,000
in US currency (other estimates vary, but not significantly). What all
experts agree upon is that the New Testament represents a talent as

being a large sum of money. A seventy-five-pound bag of silver is not chump change!

Based on my understanding now, I personally don't think the exact amount is important to the interpretation of this parable. What we can confidently conclude, however, is that one talent represented significant responsibility.

I don't believe Jesus is discussing money, although it could apply in principle. Rarely in a parable does Jesus actually use the exact representation of what is being discussed. He uses wheat for godly people, tares for evil people, seeds for words, thorns for the cares of life, the harvest for the end of the world, reapers for angels, and more. From the overall counsel of the New Testament, it's almost certain these talents represent *charisma*, or our entrusted gifts.

Another important point of this story is that each servant was not given the same amount. We will cover this fact in more depth later, but this is why, at times, I've already referred to our entrustments as "gifts." Some have one, others two, and still others have more.

The different amounts could also represent the magnitude of our gifts. Let's be candid; there are some people with greater gifts than others. There are many who possess the gift to sing, and they inspire all who hear them. But all who sing don't have the level of talent that Céline Dion or Andrea Bocelli possesses. So, if you back me into the corner, I would say each talent represents a certain gift or, just as easily, could represent the magnitude of a gift. Let's continue:

> The servant who received the five bags of silver began to invest the money and earned five more. The servant with two bags of silver also went to work and earned two more. But the servant who received the one bag of silver dug a hole in the ground and hid the master's money. (Matthew 25:16–18)

Let me personalize the story by assigning names to our servants. Let's call the first servant Allison, the second Bob, and the third Larry. Allison started with five and *multiplied* what was given to her and ended up with ten. Bob *multiplied* his two and ended up with four. However, Larry didn't multiply his entrusted gift but rather *maintained* it. Let's clearly spell it out:

Allison: 5 x 2 = 10

Bob: 2 x 2 = 4

Larry: 1 = 1

From this point forward, I'll personalize the scripture to the names we've given each servant.

THE JUDGMENT

Again, it is crucial to point out Jesus's emphasis of the word *long* in this parable. The story began with the description of a long trip, and once again, He states, "After a *long time* their master returned from his trip and called them to give an *account* of how they had used his money" (Matthew 25:19). The account the master requires from each steward represents the judgment each of us will face for how we used our entrusted gifts. Let's examine Allison first:

Allison, to whom he had entrusted the five bags of silver, came forward with five more and said, "Master, you gave me five bags of silver to invest, and I have earned five more."

Listen to the judgment of her master:

The master was full of praise. "Well done, my good and faithful servant. *You have been faithful* in handling this small amount,

so now I will give you many more responsibilities. Let's
celebrate together!" (Matthew 25:20–21)

This is a very important point we must not miss: The master says,
"You have been faithful." You can slice the master's response however you'd like, but there is no other interpretation: Jesus directly attributes *faithfulness* to *multiplication*. Reread the master's comments
carefully; there is nothing else Allison did that was highlighted! He
didn't say that she was steadfast, dependable, loyal, devoted, truthful,
or any other one-word definition for *faithful*. Don't misunderstand—
all these admirable attributes describe being faithful, but they are not
mentioned or emphasized. He also didn't point out any other virtue,
action, or result of her stewardship, only that she had multiplied.
Therefore, he directly links *faithfulness* with *multiplication*!
    The same is true with Bob. Read closely his account:

Bob, who had received the two bags of silver, came forward
and said, "Master, you gave me two bags of silver to invest, and
I have earned two more."

Along the same lines, hear the judgment of his master:

The master said, "Well done, my good and faithful servant. *You
have been faithful* in handling this small amount, so now I will
give you many more responsibilities. Let's celebrate together!"
(Matthew 25:22–23)

Once again, Jesus directly identifies *faithfulness* with *multiplication*. There is nothing else—neither action, virtue, nor result—highlighted! Jesus doesn't want the master's emphasis diluted; there is only

one takeaway: This man multiplied what was entrusted to him and it's clearly equated to being faithful.

Also, the praise Bob receives is exactly, word for word, what was stated to Allison. This reveals that on judgment day our multiplication "score" will be based on our labor. Jesus will be equally pleased with us regardless of how many or the magnitude of our gifts. All that will matter is, did we multiply?

An example would be the stay-at-home mother who multiplied her effectiveness. She will be as equally praised as the entrepreneur who multiplied his business and his giving to the kingdom.

Now let's turn our attention to Larry:

Then *Larry* with the one bag of silver came and said, "Master, I knew you were a harsh man, harvesting crops you didn't plant and gathering crops you didn't cultivate. I was afraid I would lose your money, so I hid it in the earth. Look, here is your money back." (Matthew 25:24–25)

Before moving on to Larry's judgment, let's point out some important facts. First, Larry didn't multiply; he maintained what was entrusted to him. Also, notice the reason why he didn't multiply: First, he didn't know the character of his master, so he incorrectly perceived him as harsh. Through the years of ministering to believers from different parts of the world and all walks of life, I've noticed that one of their primary stumbling blocks to fruitfulness is not knowing God's nature. (I'll cover this in depth in a later chapter.)

When we perceive Him incorrectly, it often fosters what's behind failure to multiply—*fear*. Larry was afraid! Fear, timidity, or intimidation will shut down the genuine gifts of God on our lives. This is so important and cannot be stressed enough. I know this firsthand, as I suffered with this for years. (I will also cover this in depth in a later chapter.)

Now let's look at Larry's judgment:

But the master replied, "You *wicked* and *lazy* servant!"
(Matthew 25:26)

Wow! Let's pause and examine this statement before continuing. Remember all three, not only Allison and Bob, but also Larry are *servants*; they are not *outsiders*. It is *their* master who is assessing their labor. Larry doesn't hear, "Well done, good and faithful servant," like the other two. Instead, he hears, "Wicked and lazy servant!" This is definitely an attention-grabber. Jesus is not talking about salvation, but rather the judgment of how we handle our gifts—either being rewarded or suffering loss for our labor.

Let's look at both of the master's stern words carefully. We'll start with the easier one to swallow. The Greek word for *lazy* is *oknērós*. This word is defined as, "to delay, slow, tardy, slothful, lazy."[8] Another lexicon defines it as, "pertaining to shrinking from or hesitating to engage in something worthwhile, possibly implying lack of ambition."[9]

My friend Rick Renner, who is an expert in the Greek language, says of *oknērós*, "It carries the idea of a person who has a do-nothing, lethargic, lackadaisical, apathetic, indifferent, lukewarm attitude toward life." From these three sources, we see the Greek definition enlarges our scope and brings more insight.

If you're fearful, you'll hesitate or refrain from engaging in an activity that should or could be done. If you are lethargic, you'll lack the drive to accomplish what should be done. If you're apathetic, you won't care enough to even consider acting. All scenarios do apply to this Greek word, but the servant confessed, "I was afraid." The other aspects of laziness could have come into play for this servant, but in the end, hesitation from fear was the overriding factor.

Have you ever felt the urge to do something—you just couldn't shake it, especially when in prayer—but you faltered too long because you feared failing? Then you watched someone else do it? Afterward you thought to yourself, *I had that idea and should've acted on it.* This is Jesus's point regarding this servant. He hesitated and hesitated, not just once or twice, but he hesitated the entire period of his stewardship. It's acceptable a time or two, since we usually grow from these situations. But if we flirt with hesitation long enough, it can become a pattern that ultimately leads to complete avoidance and to an unfruitful stewardship.

When the Lord first asked me to write, I hesitated for ten months. I was afraid of writing. I had failed time and time again in school. I had a classmate in college who criticized my writing in front of everyone! An aspect of one assignment was to read each other's papers, and during class discussion, my classmate vocalized his disapproval of my work to the professor. I was the only student who received criticism from a fellow classmate.

My fear of writing was well-founded: I had terrible SAT and ACT scores, numerous teachers' negative critiques, poor grades, and a critical classmate; history wasn't on my side. All of this only confirmed my hesitation. To write a book would take an enormous amount of time, and time is crucial. It would pull me away from other efforts to grow our young ministry. I had to lay these significant fears and concerns aside in order to obey His directive.

What if I had hesitated too long and didn't obey? The outcome would have been exactly as God had spoken through the two ladies I mentioned earlier. He would have given the talent to someone else, an "Allison," so to speak, who would have fulfilled the mission. She would have received my assignment. Then, where would I be today? Would I have ended up being called "lazy" before the judgment seat?

I didn't realize my destiny was wrapped up in writing! If you had said to me during my twenties, "John, God will send you to the nations of the world through your books," I would have said, as I was laughing you out of the room, "You've lost your mind! I can't even write a three-page paper." But now the books are national and international best sellers, in over one hundred languages, and number in the tens of millions. What if I had not obeyed? What if I had allowed fear to hold me back? I shudder to think of the extent of my lost opportunity!

Now, let's focus on the more difficult word spoken by the master to the third servant. The word *wicked* may seem too intense, but Jesus never used words carelessly. The Greek word for *wicked* is *ponērós*. It is defined as "possessing a serious fault and consequently being worthless."[10]

In regard to how Larry handled what was entrusted to him, this definition fits. It's no different than Paul concluding "woe is me" if he would have been unfaithful to the gift of God on his life. Larry's misguided view of his master's character was a serious fault that fueled his fear. He was *worthless* to the operation of his entrusted gift. These are very strong statements; nevertheless, if you compare Paul's words of potential non-use of his gift with Larry's behavior, they ring true.

Let me clearly summarize that this is not in regard to our salvation, but rather in how we handle our entrusted gifts. God's view is that:

> *Those who multiply are good and faithful.*
> *Those who simply maintain possess*
> *a serious fault, are worthless and lazy.*

Could it be that our view of faithfulness is incomplete? Consider this example: There's a businessman who lives in an area with a strong and expanding economy. The business, a small shop that the owner inherited from his father, is profitable but not growing. The man has had opportunities to open new branches of the business in other parts of the city, but despite his entrepreneurial gift, he has been content to "stay comfortable."

Now, let me push the envelope. In light of Larry's judgment in the parable, let's ask two important questions. Should this businessman use his gift to start new shops and venture into other markets for the purpose of building the kingdom? Is his desire to "play it safe" synonymous with the unfaithful servant's strategy "to maintain"?

Have we used the same criteria to assess faithfulness as Jesus uses? Although the businessman is living a good life, isn't the overarching question supposed to be: Is he multiplying or maintaining his gifts? Let's be honest in our assessment. Do we measure faithfulness only by reliability without factoring in reproduction? Steadiness apart from expansion? Consistency without attention to duplication? Have we missed the full scope of what it means to be faithful—to multiply whatever gifts we've been given?

God's first commandment to mankind when He placed male and female on the earth was, "Be fruitful and multiply" (Genesis 1:28). Of course, He was directing us to have babies and populate the earth. But also, and so much more, the command is this: *Whatever He puts in our care, we are to return to Him multiplied.* We are to procreate through multiplication. In the parable of the talents, Jesus specifically applies this initial Genesis command to our entrusted gifts.

NOT YOUR OWN ABILITY!

Are you feeling uncomfortable? You probably are, but remember, God's grace is all you need. You aren't asked to do this in your own strength, but by the *charis* and *charisma* of God. The purpose of writing this message is not to discourage you, but to bring awareness to your God-given potential and to expand your faith in God's grace and the gifts on your life. I don't intend to put a heavy burden—too difficult to lift—on you. Paul cried out to God three different times to ease his load, but look how the Lord responds:

> "My grace is all you need. My power works best in weakness." So now I am glad to boast about my weaknesses, so that the power of Christ can work through me. That's why I take *pleasure* in my weaknesses. (2 Corinthians 12:9–10)

One of the definitions of the Greek word for *weakness* is "limitations." You and I are not the only ones who feel overwhelmed at times. We all have limitations, as did even the apostle Paul. In the specific context of this verse, he refers to the resistance, opposition, and even physical persecutions he faced in every city (see chapter 11), but this truth also applies to restrictions or impossibilities we may face—when the task seems undoable. Although it's certainly not easy, this should cause us to deepen our resolve, to lean into His strength. Instead of *listening* to the limitations screaming in your mind, *speak* the promises of God. Do we listen to ourselves too much when, instead, we should be speaking to ourselves?

Paul asked God to intervene three times, and each time God reminded Paul of *charis*. Paul got it the third time; he realized his constraints should only steer him to believe in God's grace and gifting on his life. This is why his tune changed from, "God, take this away!" to, "I take *pleasure* in my limitations." Did he really say "pleasure"? Yes! He now realized the more impossible the challenge, the greater God's power would manifest in and on his life—*if he believed!*

Here is an important truth: *The grace we need to multiply can only be accessed by believing!* Paul writes, "We have access *by faith* into this grace" (Romans 5:2 NKJV). Imagine it this way: Faith is the pipeline that delivers to our heart the needed grace to multiply. When we hear this message, our faith or pipeline should enlarge, not diminish. But that's your choice. We are told:

> The word which they heard *did not profit them*, not being
> mixed with faith in those who heard it. For we who have
> believed do *enter that rest*. (Hebrews 4:2–3 NKJV)

Don't view what you're reading in an *unprofitable* way; instead, mix it with faith. The very same Word from God accomplished two different things for the children of Israel. It was *profitable* to Moses, Joshua, and Caleb; they were strengthened by seeing it in a positive light. But the same Word was *unprofitable* to the other Israelites because they viewed it in a negative way. This is the difference between belief and unbelief.

Believe that God has equipped you to go far beyond your own ability. He has given you no other option for strength and empowerment than to depend on His grace. When you do this, you will *enter into the true rest*—ceasing in your own efforts, no longer striving to produce results. What is this *rest*? It is to cooperate with God's ability to accomplish your mission. When you enter rest, God will lead you to multiply!

This is one reason why David was called a "man after God's heart." He depended on God's strength, not his own. He repeatedly proclaimed, "The LORD is the strength of my life" (Psalm 27:1 NKJV). In everything he accomplished, there was one common denominator: He depended on God's ability in and through him. This is why Paul says to his spiritual son, Timothy, who was battling fear and intimidation, "You therefore, my son, be *strong in the grace* that is in Christ Jesus" (2 Timothy 2:1 NKJV).

This is why I devoted the second and third chapters of this book to firmly establish *charis* and *charisma* before discussing Jesus's parable of the talents. It would be overwhelming and discouraging to face our stewardship in our own strength.

Please, don't ever forget: Your calling is greater than your natural ability. Could this be why we are told:

> For you see *your calling*, brethren, that not many wise accord-ing to the flesh, not many mighty, not many noble, *are called.* But God has chosen the foolish things of the world to put to shame the wise, and God has chosen the weak things of the world to put to shame the things which are mighty; and the base things of the world and the things which are despised God has chosen, and the things which are not, to bring to nothing the things that are, that no flesh should glory in His presence. (1 Corinthians 1:26–29 NKJV)

Why is this? Why are there only a few wise, strong, and noble who are called? Could it be that it's easier for the naturally talented to "succeed" in their own strength? They are foolish! They compare themselves to others, and they win. Instead, they should see them-selves in the light of their Creator's calling.

Paul was different. Although in measuring himself to his contem-poraries he was wise and noble before being saved, there came a point when he counted all of this natural ability to be "dung" so that he could enter into the power of Christ upon his life. He was one of the few, be-cause he learned that even though he was naturally wiser than most, he was unwise in comparison to God's wisdom (see Philippians 3:4–11).

SOCIALISTIC OR CAPITALISTIC?

Let's continue on with Jesus's parable. It may not seem possible, but it actually gets stronger and more shocking!

Then he ordered, "Take the money from this servant, and give it to the one with the ten bags of silver." (Matthew 25:28)

Okay, wait a minute! Did we just read this correctly? He actually orders the bag of silver (talent) to be taken from Larry and given to Allison. Let's spell this out clearly:

Allison: 5 x 2 = 10 + 1 (from Larry) = 11

Larry: 1 – 1 (to Allison) = 0

Allison ends up with eleven and Larry ends up with zero!

One morning in prayer, I was stunned by what I heard in my heart. Let me set this up. I actually had not thought about the parable of the talents for some time. That morning I heard the Spirit of God say to me, "Son, I'm more capitalistic, not socialistic, in My thinking."

What?! I raised an eyebrow to His words, but I've been walking with Him long enough to know when He reveals things to us that we don't know. Often it sounds contrary to religious or normal thinking, and sometimes it even sounds absurd! This time it seemed absurd when I heard His words. I asked for understanding because I thought—if anything—God was more socialistic in the way He did things.

That morning, He led me to this parable and showed me that if His thinking were socialistic, this parable would have gone differently. The story would have begun like this: All three would have received the same number of talents:

Allison: 3

Bob: 3

Larry: 3

Allison and Bob would have been faithful (multiplied), but Larry—because of his faults of being worthless and lazy—would have stayed true to form. The result would have been:

Allison 3 x 2 = 6

Bob 3 x 2 = 6

Larry 3 = 3

The hypothetical, socialistic God would have done the following:

Allison 6 − 1 = 5

Bob 6 − 1 = 5

Larry 3 + 1 (from Allison)

       + 1 (from Bob) = 5

Everyone would have ended up with five talents! But this is not what happened. God removed the one bag of silver from Larry and gave it to the one who had ten. Why? Jesus explains:

> To those who use well what they are given (*multiply*), *even more will be given*, and they will have an *abundance*. But from those who do nothing (*maintain*), even what little they have will be taken away. (Matthew 25:29)

I'm not saying that God is a capitalist. No, never! It's just that capitalism, particularly here, is more in line with His thinking and ways than socialism. Our young people in America and elsewhere in the twenty-first century are being trained to think socialistically. Socialism is not godly and beneficial; in fact, it goes directly against the wisdom of God. It is an antichrist spirit, masking as the common good, that wants to reward laziness and penalize diligence, success, and abundance.

God's way is to reward those who multiply with more, and He has no problem with them having an *abundance*. Again Jesus says, "They will have an *abundance*." God desires us to have abundance *as long as our heart is to build the kingdom and use our abundance for others.*

You've probably heard this statement before: *God is not against abundance; He is against abundance having us.* This is a very true statement. To those whose hearts burn with God's passions, their satisfaction doesn't come from hoarding abundance. Rather, it comes from walking with God and using the abundance He gives to build His kingdom. The abundance is only a tool for them to build others. And, obviously, if we are wise, we will not fall in love with our tools.

It's important to pause and stress an important truth: We are to take care of the poor—those who are incapable of labor or those who need a kick start. Paul writes, "Love empowers us to fulfill the law of the Anointed One as we carry each other's troubles. If you think you are too important to stoop down to help another, you are living in deception" (Galatians 6:2–3 TPT).

When the leaders of the early church met, they realized what their different assignments were and even disagreed on minor points. But they certainly agreed on a responsibility to help those who were struggling. Paul writes:

> They simply requested one thing of me: that I would remember the poor and needy, which was the burden I was already carrying in my heart. (Galatians 2:10 TPT)

With this stated, it is important to identify whether someone is in *need* or just *lazy*. A socialist approach is to give equally to the lazy and the poor. If we give to those in the "lazy" category, we only increase their dependence on us. Our goal is always to direct people to their God-given gifts, so they too can flourish and build God's kingdom.

THE PRACTICAL APPLICATION

In any case, what is important is the fact that we have been entrusted with gifts and we are expected to use them to multiply. If you love God, you will passionately desire to use your gifts for His glory. My main intent is to awaken you to your inward desire and potential. You have been created on purpose for a purpose. You have the capability to multiply what you've been given for the glory of our King. This is the most important takeaway from this chapter.

Now that we've come to an understanding of the parable of the talents and what it represents, we are ready to move on to the practical matters. How does this play out? How does this translate into everyday life?

Our journey will turn in this direction in the next chapter.

REFLECT

1. There's one attribute that clearly defines a steward: faithful. How have you viewed faithfulness? After reading this chapter, how has your perspective changed?

2. Eternal multiplication is not achieved in our own strength. It's a result of cooperating with God's grace. Are you attempting to multiply your gifts in your own strength? How can you multiply your gifts from a posture of rest, rather than of striving?

3. God is not against abundance; He's against abundance having us. Why do you think it's important to God that you multiply your gifts? How can the multiplication of your gifts honor God and impact others on a greater scale?

The one who manages the little he has been given with faithfulness and integrity will be promoted and trusted with greater responsibilities.

—Luke 16:10 TPT

6

Diligence and Multiplication

ccording to the words of Jesus, if we live by integrity and are steadfast, dependable, trustworthy, honest, diligent, and multiply what we currently manage, we will be given greater responsibilities. Simply put, *when we multiply with integrity, God entrusts us with more responsibility*. He promotes us. It is a law of His kingdom.

Do a personal checkup. Do you have a multiplying outlook? Or have you carried more of a maintenance mentality? Have you coasted when you hit the level of success you viewed as higher than most, better than your parents, or enough for you to live comfortably?

Be honest in your assessment. If you have been more of a maintainer, rather than a multiplier, the great news is this: You still live on the earth and have time to change, multiply, and ultimately be given more responsibility!

TWO DIFFERENT OUTCOMES

Even when I was a young boy, it wasn't hard for me to recognize these two opposite motivations of maintainer or multiplier, because my two grandfathers exemplified the differences right before my eyes. One retired at the age of sixty-five and entered into a docile lifestyle. He'd visit our home two weeks a year, and I would observe him, day by day, do practically nothing. He would sit under our big oak tree in the backyard and smoke his pipe. It wasn't much different when we visited him at his home. Sadly, in his later years, he seemed to have settled for existing, rather than living.

My other grandfather retired at the age of sixty-two and started what seemed like his second life. In his sixties, he attended Rutgers University and studied agriculture. Over the next couple of decades, he wrote two books, built and maintained a large garden, raised animals, helped bring condominiums to the Florida beaches to create nice places for older people, and was active in many corporate and community projects. He always reached out to help anyone who was in need.

When he visited us or we visited him, it was a much-anticipated event. He planned fishing trips, days at amusement parks, and trips to New York City. He played games with us, took us to meet neighbors, helped local businessmen with tasks in their shops, and every night he cooked us a delicious meal. My other grandfather didn't even help around the kitchen.

One grandfather died at the age of seventy-five and the other at the age of ninety-one. Can you guess who lived longer? Yes, the one who had a vision, the one who multiplied. Here's the interesting fact: It wasn't until he was eighty-nine years old that he received salvation. Even so, beforehand he still lived according to God's principles—the laws of the kingdom—and was abundantly blessed.

Before I had the privilege of leading him to Jesus, my grandfather persecuted me a lot about my beliefs! He mocked my faith almost every time we were together. After numerous attempts to share the gospel with him, I almost fell over when he finally said, "I want to receive Jesus as my Lord." It was a great day!

One month after his conversion, I again visited him. At the time, he only lived an hour away from our house. He had just moved from his condominium on Daytona Beach to an adult assisted living center in Ormond Beach. On that visit, he said, "John, would you like to know my assignment? What I'm on this earth to do?"

I was amazed that a newly saved man at his age thought this way. But rather than go there, I simply responded, "Yes, Grandpa, what is your assignment?"

He said with a smile, "The Holy Spirit told me I'm here to tell all these people about Jesus Christ." (There were several hundred elderly people in his complex.)

Two years later, my mom and her brother moved him to Oklahoma to be close to his only son. The first week there, he stayed up all night telling his newly assigned nurse his life story. In the wee hours of the morning, just before sunrise, he said to her, "It's time to go home. Tell my son to have a party on me." With that, he left his body and joined his heavenly family.

My mom was troubled and concerned that they had put too much stress on him with the move from Florida to Oklahoma. When she said this, I quickly assured her that they had done no such thing: "Mom, when Grandpa was eighty-nine, he told me God showed him that he had two more years on earth to fulfill his assignment in Ormond Beach. This was his first week in Oklahoma; his assignment was complete."

My mother was both comforted and amazed.

Although my grandfather was an unsaved man, God's principles of diligent faithfulness manifested in his life. In witnessing the different choices of my two grandfathers, even before I was a believer, I had determined my life would follow the course of my grandfather who multiplied and lived with purpose until his very last breath.

But let me be frank. Numerous times the temptation to veer the other way—to a life of ease—has arisen. It takes intentional redirecting of our thoughts to not succumb to the "maintainer" lifestyle because it is so much easier.

Multiplication will not manifest out of a slothful, hesitant, careless, or apathetic motivation. We are told by the apostle Paul, "Never be lazy, but *work hard* and serve the Lord *enthusiastically*" (Romans 12:11).

First of all, realize this is a command, not a suggestion. Look at his words, "work hard." In order to multiply, this is one of the first traits you must exhibit. Not only are we to *work hard*, but we are to be *enthusiastic* in our labor. Don't get me wrong—faith, vision, and perseverance are three very important factors to multiplying. But they are of no use without good, old-fashioned hard work!

Lisa and I have worked diligently almost from the day we became believers. It's hardwired within us, and God does the same for every believer. Our enthusiasm has not been driven by external circumstances, but a deep passion stemming from two things: Our unfaltering love for Jesus and for His people. This passion is based on a firm heart decision, not feelings, and it fuels the burning desire to build His kingdom. This is so important, because excited emotions will not always be present. In fact, seasons may come in which feelings aren't present at all.

One of the root words for *enthusiasm* is the Greek word *entheos*, which means "having God within."[11] Our diligence must be driven by drawing from His indwelling presence, not emotions or external circumstances.

MULTIPLY WHAT BELONGS TO ANOTHER

After we got married, the first church Lisa and I attended was in Dallas, Texas. It was one of the most recognized churches in our nation with a staff of hundreds. As volunteers, we constantly signed up to do anything that was needed. I became an usher, volunteered for prison ministry, ministered in detention centers, visited nursing homes, helped in conferences, assisted church employees with menial tasks, and even gave our pastor's children tennis lessons. I never said "no" to any form of serving, no matter what it was, and all of this happened while I was working forty hours a week as an engineer with Rockwell International.

Eventually upon seeing my passion to serve, the senior pastor's wife (who was the church's COO) asked me if I would be willing to join the church staff on a full-time basis. During our formal interview, she said, "John, I don't think we can afford you."

My response was, "Yes, you can afford me." I didn't care what they offered me. I was ready to accept any position for any salary. After the interview, she offered the position of assistant to the executive team. Lisa and I didn't need to pray too hard about it because we knew this was God's will. I accepted the offer with a salary of $18,000 a year, which was a massive pay cut, but we felt it was a promotion. Lisa and I knew we would need miraculous provision to live off this new salary, but we didn't care. We were engaged in, what we believed with all our heart, was the calling on our lives.

This position's responsibilities were to assist my pastors, their family, and their guests. I operated with three predominate motives. First, to serve them as though I was serving Jesus. Second, to always look ahead, anticipate their needs, and meet them before being asked. Finally, if asked to do something, to not come back and say, "It can't be done." I would always find a way to get it done through prayer, creativity, and hard work. If (and it was rare) something couldn't be done, I would always return with the best alternate solution. Often it was even a better way of getting the task accomplished than what was asked originally.

Lisa and I didn't have children during this position's tenure. A work-week was usually fifty to seventy hours in a six-day period. She and I both felt it was important to take all possible pressures off our pastors. We wanted them to give their full attention to leading our church.

I could share many stories that illustrated our motives but will offer just one. My pastor had a guest who was on the ministry team of a now deceased, world-renowned evangelist. My pastor wanted to learn more about the deceased evangelist, so the two of them talked late into the evening. My phone rang at 1:00 a.m. It was my pastor asking me to come to his home (a twenty-five-minute drive from our apartment) and take his guest back to the hotel.

"I'll be right over," I said without hesitation.

I went to the house and waited as they said good-bye and drove the guest back to the hotel. I got to bed well after 2:00 a.m.

My pastor was unaware that I had an airport run to pick up another guest who was speaking to our church the next evening. He was flying in that same morning on a red-eye flight from Hawaii that landed at 5:40 a.m. I had to get up at 4:30 in order to pick him up. I never told my pastor about getting less than three hours of sleep that night. I was determined to fill any need they had, and I constantly reminded myself that it was a privilege to serve.

After serving my pastor and his wife as their assistant for four years, one day when alone with them, I shared, "I am praying and asking God that the man who takes my place will do twice as good of a job that I have done." I wanted to leave well and see my position carried on even stronger.

"That's not possible," they responded. "You have done such great work."

It was an encouraging affirmation. Their statement made all the hard work seem easy, but I wanted improvement. Eventually, they put two people in the position. My pastor released us with blessings to go serve another well-known church in Florida—the youth pastor position I mentioned in chapter 2.

When I took the Florida position, I was frustrated that we weren't reaching more teenagers. This was the mid-1980s when our only visual medium was broadcast television. There were no computers, tablets, or smartphones. Streaming hadn't been invented. Simply put, daily broadcast TV was the best avenue to reach people.

After doing some research, I discovered that one of the most powerful television stations in central Florida had an open 10:00 p.m. slot on Saturday night. I inquired how much it would cost to buy that thirty-minute time slot. It was hefty.

I approached my senior pastor and asked if we could buy it for a youth outreach program. "John, it just isn't in the church's budget," he said.

I asked him, "Do you mind if we allow the teenagers the opportunity to give monthly in order to pay for the program?"

"Sure, if they can afford it," he responded. I don't think he believed the young people could do it.

I stood up before the young people and shared the vision of reaching the lost. In those days, many young people watched television late on Saturday night. On this program, we would first preach the Word of God, and then invite the viewers to attend the church and youth group. I appealed to the young people in our group to give from their allowances, after-school jobs, or to create odd jobs. When the pledges were tallied up, my assistant youth pastor and I were amazed—the cost of the TV time would be covered.

My senior pastor was even more amazed. He gave permission and we started our program, Youth Aflame. We met the budget every month, and the exciting part was that many unchurched young people started attending the youth group and came to Jesus. People have approached me more than twenty years later, sharing that back in the late 1980s they had watched Youth Aflame and how much it impacted their lives.

When I left the youth pastor position, we divided up the youth group into three different branches. The three leaders were now doing what we'd begun with one. Again, the grace of God, obedience, and hard work had fostered multiplication.

Jesus says:

> If you have not been faithful in what is another man's, who will give you what is your own? (Luke 16:12 NKJV)

Let's restate His words according to the parable of the talents:

> If you have not multiplied what is another man's, who will give you what is your own to multiply?

It was this senior pastor who declared God's plan for Lisa and me to launch Messenger International. He brought it up first, not us. When starting my tenure as youth pastor, I had said, "Pastor, I will remain here until Jesus returns for me unless God shows both you and me that we are supposed to move on." If God had not prompted him in prayer about what our next place of ministry should be, I'm not sure we would have felt free to leave the church. I believe to this day that this was the reason God showed him first.

BIRTHING OF MESSENGER INTERNATIONAL

Shortly after leaving the church in Florida, we were ministering in Columbia, South Carolina. It was early in the morning, and I had found a remote place to pray. God spoke to me: "Son, you will reap a large harvest from the faithful seeds you've sown these past seven years in serving others' ministries. It will begin immediately and continue on for years to come."

Now in looking back, I'm in awe of that harvest.

After we were launched by our church to birth Messenger International, diligence was again a key factor in our multiplying. Lisa and I spent many evenings laboring with tasks such as duplicating cassette tapes, making labels, and assembling message series. We'd have friends over on a regular basis to label and batch our newsletter or help in other areas. Lisa and I typed letters, deposited checks, kept financial records, and performed all the necessary paperwork. We made computer entries, post office runs, and supply runs—and that's the short list. We would begin working after prayer in the morning and would often labor until 9:00 p.m. or later at night.

We did it with joy and considered it a privilege. Our motivation came from within, and it endured through countless disappointments and dry times. I believe the strength to not lose heart came from the time spent in prayer each morning.

We'd travel up and down I-95, the main highway on the East Coast, in our Honda Civic with two infant boys in their car seats in the back, and preach to small churches of eighty to one hundred people. Our first meeting was actually a church that met in a funeral home—what a glamorous start!

We would sell our cassettes and use the proceeds to expand the ministry. We made a commitment that these funds couldn't pay our salary; it was important to grow and multiply Messenger. There were times when the funds we needed personally came in the exact day they were required. We had money in our "audio resource sales" account, but we had committed not to touch it.

It was after a year and a half of hard work that the word from God came that I should write. I was so concerned that there just wasn't enough time in a day to write and fulfill so many other responsibilities. It seemed risky to make the commitment, but we did. And it took quite a while to write the first book. What I didn't anticipate were a few young men who volunteered to help us with those menial tasks that would have pulled me away from writing. They stepped into the same role we'd taken with our pastor in Dallas. They saw a need in our lives and came forward without us asking.

I finished the manuscript for *Victory in the Wilderness* after a year of hard, and sometimes frustrating, work. I learned this important key: *We must grow in the grace (gifts) on our life.* Most of us don't have "fantastic" results at the beginning. Peter writes, "Grow in the grace . . . of our Lord and Savior Jesus Christ" (2 Peter 3:18 NKJV). My ability to write now is so much more developed than when I wrote the first book.

Lisa and I submitted the manuscript to a well-known editor. To my utter shock, he sharply criticized it, stating I was too young and inexperienced to bring such a message to the body of Christ.

After that blow of rejection, Lisa and I immediately sought another editor. We found one, and he proceeded to botch the entire manuscript. Lisa and I were devastated when we got it back. He'd lost my voice and the strong impact of the content. And, worse, it didn't make much sense! Simply put, it had been butchered. Yet, another blow—what would we do? It had already been more than a year.

We didn't give up. We found another editor, and after she read it, agreed that the original manuscript had been ruined. "John and Lisa," she said, "often it's not the right course of action to fix a botch. Take the loss on what you paid the editor and start over." She recommended that Lisa edit the original and then send it to her.

We took the editor's advice, and Lisa spent hours on the original manuscript, improving the readability of the message. The new editor then took Lisa's finished edits and began her process. She did an amazing job, and we felt as if we finally had a great manuscript.

I submitted it to two well-known publishing houses. We never heard from one of them, but the other responded. They stated that my book was too "preachy," and since I was not a well-known minister, they would not publish it. I tried to get it placed with other lesser-known publishers, but no one was interested.

Can you imagine our disappointment? Now, after well over a year's worth of work and time, it seemed we were at a dead end. I was distraught, but not willing to quit.

Self-publishing was practically unheard of in those days. No one successful in publishing had done it, but a friend suggested we give it a try. We learned it would cost us $12,000 to print a few thousand books, and that didn't include the cost of artwork and typesetting; and we had already paid two editors.

This was a massive sum of money for us. Messenger International's entire income for 1990 was $40,000. We were beginning our third year as a ministry, and we weren't bringing in too much more than what we had brought in that first year. Toward the end of our second year, I remember feeling overwhelmed when purchasing our first computer, which cost only a few hundred dollars—$12,000 seemed impossible! We needed a miracle to come up with that kind of money.

We met a lady who worked in a typesetting position for a small niche publisher that specialized in outdoor sporting books. She heard me talk about writing and approached Lisa to offer her services to typeset and compose our book at no charge. We were so happy to not have to pay thousands of dollars for this service.

God miraculously brought in the money for the rest of what was required to self-publish, and we printed five thousand *Victory in the Wilderness* books (which has since been retitled to *God, Where Are You?!*). Our initial excitement didn't last long once we realized we had no distribution channels. Distributors and bookstores had no idea who we were, and back in those days, these companies only purchased from established publishing houses. No one was interested in a self-published book.

We added the book to the cassette-tape series on our resource table and sold copies wherever we ministered. When I spoke on the topic of the wilderness, we would sell out. People loved the message, but that's as far as it went.

In prayer God spoke to me about writing another book, so I spent another nine months writing *The Voice of One Crying*. Still no publishers were interested, so again we self-published that book in 1993. Now we had two books on our resource table, but neither was available in any retail outlet.

AN OPEN-DOOR OPPORTUNITY

A year later, a friend of mine called me and asked me to lunch. "I want you to meet a friend of mine," he said.

I agreed to go. I learned it was the new leader of the publishing house that had turned me down two years earlier. The lunch went well, and the man took an interest in what Lisa and I were doing. "What is the message that you have been speaking on lately?" he asked.

I began to share the hottest topic on my heart. It was a message addressing the importance of overcoming offenses and forgiving those who'd hurt us. He continued to probe, and I told him more of the message. After fifteen minutes, he said, "John, you know we couldn't publish this because we only do twenty-two to twenty-four books a year, and those books are written by well-known authors or ministers."

I looked at him, puzzled, and said, "I wasn't trying to sell you on publishing me; you asked what I was speaking on in my travels."

He caught it and laughed. "Oh yes, that's right, keep going."

So, I continued to share. Fifteen minutes later, he interrupted me again, "Can you get me a manuscript in the next three months?"

Puzzled, I replied, "I thought you said you couldn't publish me."

"I've changed my mind," he responded. "This message needs to get into the earth."

The company released *The Bait of Satan* in June of 1994. I was so excited. God had opened a door that I couldn't open myself. I was positive it would immediately become popular and sell well; however, that didn't happen in the first seven months. Month after month, I got the discouraging sales figures from the publisher. I believed in my heart that this message was destined to go to the masses—to the nations of the world. I refused to let go of that hope, but all indicators pointed toward yet another devastating disappointment.

A few months later, I got a call from one of the publisher's marketing team members. She said, "John, there is an international live talk show that wants to have you on their program on January 16, 1995. They will allot you twenty minutes, but they primarily want to talk about you, Lisa, your four sons, and your travel ministry. However, they are willing to mention your book. It's a start; a crack in the door, so to speak. Do you want us to accept for you?"

"Definitely yes!"

I went, and it was a very well-known couple who hosted the program that evening. After he greeted me, the first thing the husband did was to hold up *The Bait of Satan* and ask, "What is the bait of Satan? What's this message about?"

I was surprised that this topic, and not our family, had come up first, but I jumped right in to speak about the book's message. It was as if everything came to a halt in the studio. I had been told to watch the floor director closely, because she would hold up signs indicating the time left in the interview. It had been emphasized that I would only have twenty minutes. The floor director didn't hold up any signs. The hosts were captivated by what I was saying and didn't interrupt, interject, or say anything. The couple and I lost track of time and later found out I had spoken nonstop for forty minutes.

The host was profoundly impacted. He had one of the largest conferences in the nation. One of the first things he did, live on air, was invite me to come and speak on this subject at their conference.

A couple of days later, the publisher informed me that every bookstore in the United States was sold out of *The Bait of Satan* and twenty thousand copies were back-ordered. "John, we've never seen this before," he said, "and the talk show has told us they've never seen such a response." I knew in my heart it was a divine setup, and it confirmed that this was God's message being promoted.

The Bait of Satan eventually became an international best seller and has been on and off the charts for the past twenty-five years. At the time of this writing, it's approaching the two million mark—in paperback, e-book, and audiobook. It's ironic to look back at how this evolved. The publisher that originally rejected me as an author now has *The Bait of Satan* as one of its top-selling books of all time. God certainly has a sense of humor!

If I would have disobeyed and not written, the message wouldn't have strengthened so many people. Writing caused the message to multiply, as the book was reaching substantially more people than I would ever have been able to speak in front of.

Actually, this profound proliferation didn't start with the writing of the book. The multiplication began much earlier, as we continued on this course through the many blows we suffered. I was working diligently to take all pressure off my first pastor and then multiplying our church's outreach as a youth pastor. It continued through Messenger International—working all hours of the day and evening and then obeying God's voice to write and publish.

I thought the multiplication process for the Bait of Satan message was established, that it would naturally continue to grow with book sales and through me sharing the message in conferences and churches globally. I was wrong. God was about to entrust us with more.

REFLECT

1. Do you have an outlook that encourages multiplication?
    Or have you carried more of a maintenance mentality?
    Are you living comfortably and just getting by, or are you
    continuing to challenge yourself?

2. Multiplication isn't realized by being lazy and passive. Not
    only are we to work hard, but we are to be enthusiastic in
    our labor. Would you consider yourself a hard worker?
    Are you enthusiastic about your work? Have you coasted
    when you achieved a level of success you viewed as suffi-
    cient or better than others?

3. When I began writing, I experienced frustration, rejec-
    tion, and discouragement; but breakthrough came as I
    remained obedient to what God had told me to do. How
    are you growing in the grace that's on your life? How does
    my story encourage you to push through frustration and
    discouragement?

By His blessing they multiply greatly.

—Psalm 107:38 ESV

7

Great Multiplication

Often God will use frustration or discontentment as a catalyst to stir our faith for either initial multiplication or the next level of multiplication. An example of this is found with Abram (Abraham). God appeared to him when he was seventy-five years of age and spoke in a vision:

> Do not be afraid, Abram, for *I will protect you*, and *your reward will be great*. (Genesis 15:1)

Let's set the stage. God Almighty is the One who created and owns all the earth, including its vast resources. He has always existed and will never end. No other being comes anywhere near His greatness. He doesn't have life; He *is* life. All enduring knowledge, wisdom, treasures, and pleasures are in Him. There's nothing of value outside of Him.

With this in mind, this awesome Being declares He will *protect* Abram and give him *a great reward*. Let's discuss both *protection* and a *great reward*.

First, *protection*. Imagine if the president of the United States assigned all the armed forces to *protect* you. All the generals inform their down-line officers that you are top priority, and anything that's required for your safety should be implemented. If needed, they will station every soldier, with their full spectrum of advanced weaponry, near you. It's almost unimaginable, but if this occurred, I'm sure you'd feel very safe and secure. But this pales in comparison to God Almighty saying, "I will *protect* you."

How about a *great reward*? If your neighbor says, "I'm going to give you a *huge* reward," that's very kind and generous, except that he may not have much to offer. If the wealthiest man in the United States makes the same statement, you would get more excited. But neither matches the case here. The One who owns everything on the planet and in the universe is offering the reward! He declares to Abram, "The reward I have for you is 'great.'" Honestly, the enormousness of this promise is difficult to grasp. And we're still not done setting up the scene.

The other mind-blowing reality is that the Creator doesn't send a messenger—He comes in person. God Almighty makes these unimaginable promises face-to-face. Can you imagine the magnitude? What would our reaction be? How can words express the excitement, joy, happiness, and awe that any of us would feel? But Abram's response isn't close to these emotions. In fact, he's not excited; he's actually frustrated!

> But Abram replied, "O Sovereign LORD, what good are all Your blessings when I don't even have a son?" (Genesis 15:2)

Do you hear the discontentment in his response? Amazing! But could Abram's lack of enthusiasm actually be a good thing? Suppose Abram had said, "Wow, this is awesome! Let's get this party started!" Would the eventual outcome have been different? In fact, the better question is, would God have even appeared to Abram if this would have been his response? I don't believe so—let me explain.

Let's pause Abram's story to bring clarity. Years later, when the Israelites were wandering in the wilderness, their discontentment stemmed from personal discomfort, which, sadly, cost them their destiny. However, the apostle Paul projected his own godly attitude in stating:

> I have learned how to be content with whatever I have. I know how to live on almost nothing or with everything. I have learned the secret of living in every situation, whether it is with a full stomach or empty, with plenty or little. (Philippians 4:11–12)

In both Paul and Abram, God found someone willing to embrace hardship and look beyond themselves. Their dissatisfaction wasn't personal, but rather focused on others.

Here's a good rule of thumb: If discontentment stems from what I personally lack, it is displeasing to God. On the other hand, if discontentment focuses on the needs of others and building the kingdom, it's pleasing to God. This was Abram's frustration, and what became of it? God enlarged his vision by highlighting the stars of the heaven and the sands of the seashore, promising his reward would impact more than he could number. It moved God to declare, "I will make My covenant between Me and you, and will *multiply you exceedingly*" (Genesis 17:2 NKJV).

What if Abram had been content with his own life being remarkably blessed? Would he, at age seventy-five, have had a reason to believe that he could father a child? *His dissatisfaction became the catalyst to multiply.*

I've learned that this discontentment is not something to ignore but is a springboard to increased effectiveness. It's what the church in the city of Laodicea lacked. Jesus sternly corrected them for their attitude of "I . . . have need of nothing" (Revelation 3:17 NKJV). They didn't feel frustrated when they didn't see others being impacted, because they were self-focused and comfortable in their plenty. Consequently, they didn't seek to multiply.

This describes the temptation that Stan wrestled with. I, at times, struggle with this also and have had to fight it off. In fact, almost all or most of us do.

The longer I serve God, the more I've come to realize that one of the genuine fruits of a true believer is a deep passion to impact others for the kingdom. At the moment of our salvation, we are changed into a completely different person. We are reborn with a driving passion to serve. Jesus states:

> Be *dressed for service* and keep your *lamps burning.* (Luke 12:35)

This charge from our Master highlights the posture that all believers are to maintain: *service* and the *passion* to serve. I chose the word *maintain,* because it's already a part of our new nature. This is often overlooked due to our fear of slipping over to "works" to be saved, as opposed to salvation being a free gift. However, this is not at all the case; it's our spirit's inborn desire to serve. Why would we avoid discussing or dumbing down this huge aspect of our new life? Could it be that the desire to reinvent Christianity is to become more of a consumer-based faith experience? Are we appealing to the spiritual laziness of humanity's fallen nature?

Why would Jesus say, "Be dressed for service"? Why does He couple clothing with service? The book of Revelation gives us a clue:

> "Let us be glad and rejoice, and let us give honor to Him. For the time has come for the wedding feast of the Lamb, and His bride has *prepared herself.* She has been given the finest of pure white linen to wear." For the fine linen represents *the good deeds* of God's holy people. (Revelation 19:7–8)

First, we see that the bride, not God, has prepared herself. Second is the manner in which she has prepared herself. Every bride takes a lot of time to pick out her wedding attire. It is one of her most important to-do-list items for the big day. In our Western culture, she spends considerable time *shopping for and buying* the outfit. In the kingdom of God, being the bride of Christ, we spend considerable time *making* our outfit. Our attire is constructed from fine linen, which according to the previous Scripture is our service in building the kingdom. Thus, serving is in our spiritual DNA. Jesus says, "As the Father has sent Me, so I am sending you" (John 20:21). He came for the purpose to serve (see Mark 10:45), and our mandate is no different. He also gives the "why" behind the importance of serving: "My nourishment comes from doing the will of God, who sent me, and from finishing His work" (John 4:34).

We would not last long physically without food or nourishment. Similarly, a believer serving to build the kingdom will not last long without nourishment, and will eventually backslide. And this is the scenario Jesus describes as He continues in Luke 12. For this reason, the forces of the fallen world's system will work hard to get us to enter a comfortable and complacent outlook, instead of embracing the dissatisfaction that leads to multiplication.

So, dear reader, don't despise discontentment over the level of your impact! It's most often God's way of stirring your faith to believe for divine multiplication.

MY DISCONTENTMENT

Once *The Bait of Satan* book took off, not only in the United States but in other nations, you would think I would have been satisfied. I wasn't. I began wrestling with discontentment on another level.

I was now speaking to much larger churches and conferences, but my frustration stemmed from the inability to get the full message communicated in a single service. It takes me roughly four hundred hours to write a book, and so much is revealed by the Holy Spirit during the time of writing this book. These truths are revealed for the people God loves for the purpose of strengthening, freeing, or drawing them closer to Him.

The time allotted for a message in most churches or conferences is thirty-five to forty-five minutes. So, when speaking about *The Bait of Satan*, I could get a chapter, at best a chapter and a half, covered. This meant that ninety percent of the message was not reaching the people unless they purchased—and read—the book. This is about one-fifth of those in attendance.

Resulting from this frustration, an idea came four or five years after the book was published: Why not create a curriculum/study of the book? I could teach twelve thirty-minute video lessons and cover the critical truths in each chapter. Now people, whether in groups or individually, could get the entire message, not only by reading it but also by seeing and hearing it. This would also expand the effectiveness of the message. We could create discussion questions for groups or individuals that would give the Holy Spirit the opportunity to probe deeper and make the message more applicable to each person.

I discussed it with our team. One member suggested searching for an educational company to create a devotional student workbook, along with a leader's manual that would complement the twelve videos. This curriculum/study could be used in a wide variety of settings.

We located an excellent manufacturer that did this work for over twenty-five hundred clients, including some of the larger corporations in the United States. We requested up front that there be, "No cutting corners, no compromising quality, and be highly innovative. Let's aim to be years ahead both in style and technology." As a side note,

I was privileged to have done a Bible study for the staff of one of our US presidents. When entering the West Wing of the White House, I couldn't help but notice excellence. That day the thought came to me, *This represents the president of the United States; we at Messenger represent the King of the universe.* Even though we had stressed excellence from the beginning, after this experience, we would be even more resolute to not ever sacrifice quality or cut corners.

Once we had the curriculum/study ready to go, two team members were reassigned to work full-time on making telephone calls (it was still the best way to communicate with leaders in the early 2000s). They were instructed to contact every church we'd been to over the past ten years and inform the leaders of the curriculum/study. Our heart was to come alongside the pastors and help disciple their people, ultimately strengthening the local church. In those days, there were not that many similar curriculums available; the idea hadn't caught on.

We were so pleased when the idea resonated with leaders—the response was mind-blowing! After a short time, churches started reporting back to us that their attendance was escalating, either in small groups or in their main services. We initially thought that only churches of less than three hundred would use the curriculum for their services. However, there were a few churches with attendance in the thousands using the videos in their Sunday services. They also were growing. Leaders were reporting that their people were requesting that they not show the next lesson during an upcoming holiday weekend because they would be away. We heard of reports of churches doubling and even tripling in attendance.

Pastors shared with other pastor friends what was taking place in their churches or small groups. Now pastors were calling us, seeking to obtain the curriculum. Within a few years, we had thousands of churches involved—over twenty thousand churches in the United

States and over one thousand churches in Australia. Our church relations department grew to seven full-time members. The testimonies kept pouring into our office about lives, families, and churches being changed.

Over the next several years, we did a curriculum/study for every major book our ministry released. Within twelve years, we had over ten different curricula being used in churches all over the United States and Australia.

There was an aspect of this multiplication we didn't foresee but discovered later. A myriad of individuals, who never would have purchased a book or heard me speak, were now getting the messages. These individuals were in churches or small groups whose leaders had decided to take them through the materials.

"YOU'VE BEEN FAITHFUL"

Of course, we were filled with gratitude! The number of books sold now numbered in the millions, the curricula/studies in the hundreds of thousands. But I still wrestled with dissatisfaction. I knew these messages were for the body of Christ and were bearing much fruit, but there were still many believers in need of the truths that they carried.

I asked God for the privilege of giving away more books than were being sold. I knew there were pastors, leaders, and believers all over the globe who didn't have the finances or even the ability to purchase books. There were countless millions in underground churches whose nations wouldn't authorize the sale of Christian books. There were even more in nations who didn't have the resources to import books.

How could we help them?

I knew there was a great need, but connecting with these pastors and leaders seemed an impossible task. Nevertheless, we had to do something. We started by responding to whatever came before us. We instructed our international director that if any group of leaders in a developing or persecuted nation needed books, we would send all they needed as gifts or arrange to pay for the printing of the books in their nation.

The frustration continued to mount as we were only able to do a tiny portion: ten thousand to twenty thousand books per year. This number seemed like a drop in the bucket for satisfying the discipleship materials needed, but we continued year after year, seizing any opportunities that came before us.

Then came Memorial Day 2010 (May 31). Lisa was in England ministering at a women's conference. I had just finished playing a round of golf. I grabbed my Bible and went to our basement, feeling an urge to read the book of Daniel. While I was reading the second chapter, suddenly the Spirit of God filled our basement and I heard these words in my heart: "Son, you've been *faithful* over the English-speaking realm. Now I want you to get your messages into the hands of every pastor and leader in the world."

The presence of God lingered for several minutes. With awe and wonder, I remained still until it lifted. That day I knew there had been a shift. We would no longer merely seize opportunities that came before us, but now we had a divine commission: We would intentionally seek out pastors and leaders in need—regardless of their nation, language, or financial position.

The attention-grabber in this encounter with the Holy Spirit was the use of the word *faithful*. At that time, I didn't associate "faithful" with "multiplication"—this truth hadn't been revealed to me. If I'd been asked then what the biblical definition of faithful was, my reply never would have contained the word *multiplication*. The Spirit's words to me in the basement were the beginning of opening my heart to this understanding. I knew that I had heard from God but still questioned how our ministry could perform such a monumental task.

During this time period, we had a longtime friend, Rob Birkbeck, who worked for a famous evangelist's large international ministry. Rob was a senior director in that ministry and one of his responsibilities was to print and distribute the evangelist's books, so Rob was well connected with the publishers and pastoral networks in almost every nation of the world. Rob had just lost his position due to the evangelist's retirement. Lisa and I invited Rob and his wife, Vanessa, to join our team as we'd recently lost our international director. None of us realized the impact this partnership would foster.

It was now January 2011, and Rob and Vanessa, along with our ministry's top leaders, were meeting in our conference room. In the course of the meeting, I asked, "How many books did we give to pastors and leaders in foreign nations last year?"

One of the team members looked through the year-end summary and answered, "Thirty-three thousand books." He thought he would hear a favorable response, but it was just the opposite. My frustration spoke out: "That's pathetic!" Then I blurted, "This year we will give 250,000 books to pastors and leaders in developing and persecuted nations."

The entire room went dead silent. Lisa told me later, that at that moment, she tasted throw-up in her mouth! (She has a fabulous sense of humor!)

Finally, our COO, who happens to be our oldest son, spoke first. "Dad," Addison said, "are you sure you want to do that many?"

"Yes, we will," I wholeheartedly replied.

He proceeded to challenge me for the next twenty minutes. We kept going back and forth in front of everyone else, who remained quiet. He was very respectful but wouldn't budge from contending that my directive was too lofty. He finally blurted out in frustration, "I just don't want to give our team an unrealistic goal!"

At this point, I'd had enough. I proceeded to slam my fist down on the table and sternly declared, "I said we are going to give away 250,000 books this year." The room fell silent. Soon afterward the meeting adjourned, and we all left feeling uncomfortable.

The next morning when we were alone, my son said, "I was a bit uncomfortable with the way you spoke to me."

We were both calm now and wanting to reconcile. "Son, you know I love our team's input," I replied. "I usually weigh out everyone's suggestions and thoughts before making a final decision. However, yesterday was different. I didn't ask you all, 'Do you think we should give away 250,000 books?' Or, 'How many books do you all think we should give away next year?' I stated we were going to do this! But you argued with me for twenty minutes."

He acknowledged and agreed, but peacefully made one final appeal: "Dad, could you pray about this for twenty-four hours? If afterward you still believe we should do it, our team will put all its efforts into making this happen."

"Sure, I'll do it," I responded.

Honestly, I didn't pray much about it! I breathed a halfhearted prayer in order to keep my word, but I already knew, from my encounter in the basement, it was the right thing to do.

You may now be wondering, "Were you nervous?" You bet. I was borderline terrified! I restrained myself from going down the mental path of where the finances would come from. If I allowed myself to go down that path, I would have quickly agreed with my son and backed the number down to what seemed "reasonable." The goal of a quarter-million books seemed impossible, but I was determined to stay with the directive I'd received. I knew somehow that either a creative strategy would come or there would be miraculous provision. Little did I know, not one, but both would occur.

Three weeks later, I was in a hotel room in Florida writing a new book. Our team knows not to call me in the morning when I'm writing—it's the best time for me to concentrate. My cell phone rang and I saw on the caller ID that it was the office. I answered, as I knew it must be something either urgent or important. I heard a jovial group atmosphere on the other end. All the same people who'd been in the intense confrontational meeting three weeks earlier were in the room, and they seemed to be celebrating and laughing.

Addison said, "Dad, we haven't sent out an official communication to our financial partners about the initiative to give away 250,000 books, but one of our team members was talking to a man he knows, and when he heard about our plan, he committed to give $300,000 for this project!"

Until this moment, the largest gift our ministry had received from one individual was $50,000. Now, I joined in the celebration! After many jubilant and wonder-filled comments, I said to everyone, "Now do you understand why I was so insistent in that meeting three weeks ago?"

My son laughed and quickly said, "Dad, if you tell us to give away one million books, I'm totally on board." The others heartily agreed.

I will never forget that morning. I hung up the phone and couldn't write any longer. All I could do was pace the floor of my hotel room saying, "Thank You! Thank You! Thank You!" The entire time, tears were streaming down my face. All I could see in my heart were hungry pastors and leaders getting the discipleship resources they so desperately longed for.

I am so grateful that Addison was honest and challenged me. I'm glad he didn't keep his thoughts inside, but spoke what many others in that room felt. They most likely heard their own concerns being articulated in Addison's challenges, and these thoughts needed to be confronted. The whole drama caused us to face off with looming fears, which if listened to probably would have drawn us to change course and stay within our own means. Our vision would have withered, and we would not have received such a large, generous gift. Maybe we would have distributed fifty thousand books or remained undecided.

We set a goal and the Holy Spirit heard it, and then moved on this man's heart to give an extraordinary gift. As a team, we grew to a new level of faith.

That year, by the grace of God, we were able to give 271,700 books to pastors and leaders in forty-eight nations. Some of the nations were Iran, Iraq, Syria, Lebanon, Uzbekistan, Kazakhstan, Turkmenistan, Croatia, Albania, Egypt, Vietnam, Myanmar, Cambodia, China, Mongolia, Turkey, numerous needy African nations, and more. In previous years, we'd given tens of thousands; now it reached over a quarter of a million. Our outreach effectiveness grew over eight times. Praise God—that's great multiplication!

MORE DISCONTENTMENT

Could there be more?

In May 2011, four months after the intense confrontion in the boardroom, Rob and I were in Beirut, Lebanon, ministering to pastors and leaders who had traveled from all over the Middle East. In the midst of the meetings, Rob approached me with a request: "There is a pastor here from Irbil, Iraq, who would love to spend a little time with you. Would you like to meet with him?"

"Absolutely yes!"

Rob arranged for us to meet in the hotel lobby. The pastor was young, around thirty-five years old, and his eyes burned with passion and desire. I could tell he was serious about building the kingdom.

He was dressed for service and his lamp was blazing! He had traveled from Irbil for one reason—to be strengthened by the teaching and meetings. I could tell immediately that he was a progressive and innovative leader, understanding the importance of being relevant to the lost.

Our meeting started lightheartedly with comfortable interaction. But eventually, our conversation turned more serious and at one point he stated, "Pastor Bevere, I see you as a spiritual father. I read anything you write." (There were limited books in his language, but he could read English.) "I even use my credit card to download your materials from Messenger International's website . . ."

At that point, I checked out. Honestly, I don't remember much of anything else we discussed. My mind was screaming, *I'm looking at a pastor from the devastated, war-torn nation of Iraq, and he has to use his credit card to get materials off our website?* I couldn't wait to get alone with the Lord to address this chronic need.

After saying good-bye, I went straight to my room and closed the door. I was so frustrated, I yelled, "God, You have got to show me how to get the messages You've entrusted to us to the pastors and leaders in this world who need them." I really didn't care who was in the room next to me. I had to hear heaven's strategy for how to accomplish His commission to provide resources for these leaders.

Not many days after this intense time of prayer, an idea came. An idea came for a strategy that would cause our outreach to become more effective many times over; in fact, exponentially more effective without much additional work or expense.

It was a brilliant idea . . . and could only be the wisdom of God. So simple, yet we hadn't considered it. Read on!

REFLECT

1. Frustration or discontentment can often act as a catalyst to stir our faith for multiplication. Is God challenging you to grow in a certain area of your life? If so, how are you responding to His promptings?

2. If discontentment stems from what you lack personally, it is displeasing to God. On the other hand, if discontentment focuses on the needs of others and building the kingdom, it's pleasing to Him. What has been the focus of your discontentment?

3. Consider my story about giving away 250,000 books. Why is faith vital to laying hold of God's promises and reaching new levels of multiplication? Why is it important that you obey God, even when others don't agree with you?

If you don't know what you're doing,
pray to the Father. He loves to help.

—James 1:5 MSG

8

Strategic Ideas

With each passing year, I become more convinced of the tremendous value of an *inspired strategic idea*. Often, we look for God's provision or intervention to occur without a tactical plan, but frequently that isn't what happens. It's God-induced strategic ideas that happen! There are too many biblical illustrations to list, but let's mention a few that support this reality:

- The *strategic idea* to throw a piece of wood into the bitter water so that millions of people could drink (see Exodus 15:22–25).
- A different *inspired idea* to strike a rock, providing water for millions (see Exodus 17:5–6).
- The *strategic idea* to march once quietly around impenetrable walls of a mighty city for six days. Then on the seventh day a different *strategic idea*—to march seven times around with horns blowing and finally giving a long shout. All of this to gain entrance and conquer the city (see Joshua 6).
- The *strategic idea* to identify a military's top warriors by having tens of thousands drink water from a spring and then separating those who looked down from those who kept their eye on the battlefield (see Judges 7:4–6).
- The *strategic idea* to not attack an enemy head-on, but to circle back behind in the forest and wait to hear the marching feet in

the tops of the poplar trees, signaling the Lord's assistance in the battle (see 2 Samuel 5:22–25).

- The *strategic idea* in a severe famine to ask a widow and her son to feed the prophet with their final meal, instead of eating it themselves; by obeying, they would not starve and die as many other families did (see 1 Kings 17:8–15).

- The *strategic idea* of asking a widow in debt, who was about to lose her two sons, what she had in her house. Then instructing her to borrow empty jars from others so as to pour her only possession—a small amount of olive oil—to fill the jars; then sell the oil and pay the debt (see 2 Kings 4:1–7).

- The *strategic idea* to send a military officer with a disease to dip himself in the Jordan River seven times, resulting in his complete healing (see 2 Kings 5:1–19).

- The *strategic idea* to send the praise and worship team out ahead of the military troops, which produced a phenomenal victory (see 2 Chronicles 20:21–26).

- The *strategic idea* to eat vegetables, instead of the king's rich foods, to be healthier, better nourished, and stand out among the finest young men in the land (see Daniel 1:8–16).

- The *strategic idea* to use existing water pots and fresh water to obtain the best wine in order to save a wedding reception (see John 2:6–10).

- The *strategic idea* to take a small lunch, then blessing, breaking, and distributing it, to feed thousands of people (see Matthew 14:13–21).

- The *strategic idea* to spit and make mud and put it on the eyes of a blind man. Then telling him to go wash to restore his sight (see John 9:6–7).

- The *strategic idea* to not leave a sinking ship in order to be saved (see Acts 27:21–44).

In every case, the inspired ideas led to divine intervention. Do you see a common thread running through each event? The strategies involved using what the recipients already possessed, such as an available resource or a repositioning of themselves. In every case, the divine provision was wrapped up in the familiar. In other words, the key component leading to the miracle didn't magically appear.

God often gives strategies using the ordinary, in an unordinary way, to get extraordinary results. This highlights the importance of an inspired idea. We are told, "Getting wisdom is the most important thing you can do" (Proverbs 4:7 GNT). One form of divine wisdom is a strategic idea, and the good news is that God doesn't withhold wisdom. When we face uncommon challenges, the apostle James instructs us:

> If you need wisdom [a strategic idea], ask our generous
> God, and He will give it to you. He will not rebuke you for
> asking. (James 1:5, bracketed clarification is mine)

He'll make it plain, not holding back or hiding it from you. This is His promise. However, there are two conditions that must be met for receiving an inspired strategic idea:

> Just make sure you ask empowered by *confident faith*
> without doubting that you will receive. For the ambivalent
> person believes one minute and doubts the next. Being
> *undecided* makes you become like the rough seas driven
> and tossed by the wind. You're up one minute and tossed
> down the next. When you are *half-hearted* and *wavering* it
> leaves you unstable. Can you really expect to receive any-
> thing from the Lord when you're in that condition? (James
> 1:6–8 TPT)

We must ask with *confident faith*—we don't *hope* for the tactical idea—we fully expect it. Also, we must possess a passion for our request—we must *desperately want it*. Our request doesn't come out of a ho-hum lethargic attitude, such as, *If I receive, that's great; if not, no problem.* There is a sense of desperation and a firm determination to receive.

The *strategic idea* is a gift from God, and once received, it will open us to another realm of effectiveness. It empowers us to multiply.

AN INSPIRED, STRATEGIC IDEA

Getting back to the hotel in Beirut, I didn't go to my room and pray quietly; I just couldn't. I was at my wits' end, out of ideas, and knew I'd been entrusted with the responsibility to resource these needy and hungry pastors. I don't make a practice of yelling in hotel rooms, but honestly, that day, I didn't care who heard me. It was a desperate cry to receive the *strategy* (wisdom) to multiply our effectiveness.

After a time of intense prayer, peace filled my heart. I knew my request was heard, and experiencing relief, I now believed the answer would come. Thanksgiving poured out of my inner being, even though I still didn't have a *strategic idea* or *plan*.

A few days later, I had a thought: *We are spending a lot of time, money, and energy printing and distributing these books, but each leader is only receiving a single item. Why not do what we did in English years ago? Why not also make the full curriculum available in other languages to the leaders? We will increase all of our effectiveness!*

But there was still a huge challenge; how can we print and distribute so much material? Even if we paid to print all the contents of a curriculum, in most of the targeted nations our distributers would be responsible for more pounds of weight than they could carry, because most of the distribution occurs in jungles, mountains, deserts, or waterways that are difficult to access. Often there are no paved roads. Not only this, but in hostile nations, the carriers would be easily identified by opposing authorities and the material confiscated.

After more prayer and contemplation, another idea arose of putting the full curriculum on a DVD-ROM (a DVD disc that holds "read-only" data for a computer system). But this plan also presented questions: Do pastors and leaders in these nations have computer capabilities? If so, could their computers even read a DVD-ROM? On a totally different front: Is there enough space on a DVD-ROM to contain all the data required for a full study?

I was eager to investigate, so I first approached Rob. He was the most knowledgeable of the technical capabilities of our targeted nations since he'd been to over 160 countries. I asked him, "Do pastors and leaders in most nations, even if they are poor, have the use of computers?"

"Most do, but there are a few who don't."

"Can their computer read a DVD-ROM? And if so, how much material can we put on a DVD-ROM?"

Rob lit up and said, "Yes. And as for the second question, offhand, I would guess quite a bit!"

Then I threw out the idea, "Can we put a sleeve in the back of the book holding the DVD-ROM?"

"Yes!" he affirmed enthusiastically.

"How much more will it cost to do all this per book?"

Rob did the research and got back to me within days: "I've got great news. Looking at our average cost for printing and distributing a book, it will only cost another 5 percent to add the DVD-ROM."

I was excited but still a bit reserved, unsure of how much data could go on a disc.

"But here is the really good news," Rob said. "We can put not only the entire curriculum on the disc, but also the audiobook, two or three other books, a New Testament, and a PDF file (to print more books if the local pastor had the capability)!"

To say the least, we were jubilant and energized.

This led to another *strategic idea*. Again, it was conditional to the technical abilities of the seeded nations. I asked, "Do most in these nations have access to the internet?"

"In most nations, yes," Rob replied.

"What if we develop a website that contains all these translated resources? Let's give it a name that won't stand out as a Christian website; this way, governments opposing biblical teachings won't block it. We can print the website's location on the front page of the book and instruct the pastor/leader to encourage their people to download all these resources from the website at no cost so the entire church can go through it together."

We were like two kids in a candy store—our excitement couldn't be contained. More ideas flowed between us to help strengthen the strategy.

After completing all due diligence, we indeed determined that due to large quantities, we could manufacture and distribute these "leadership kits" for roughly four dollars each. Our team at Messenger had the skill and know-how to develop the website.

Our team soon realized that this one idea from heaven provided the potential to teach, train, and strengthen entire congregations or small groups, not just individual leaders. Many small villages throughout the world have only a single church, which means we were able to significantly impact the community for just a few dollars. What a return on investment! Could this really be possible?

At the next department head meeting at Messenger, we shared the vision. The enthusiasm caught on; each team member was ecstatic with joy and energized by the plan. I passionately declared, "It doesn't matter if it takes ten years, twenty years, or however many years, we are going to reach and help every leader on the planet with our God-entrusted resources."

One month later, a businessman from Texas called our office. He requested a fifteen-minute meeting with Lisa and me. He and his wife flew to Colorado. During our meeting, he began to weep. Through his tears, he trembled and said, "I know what you're doing! I know you are strengthening pastors in remote places with your resources. I want to be a part of this." He then slid a check across the table. I almost fell out of my chair; it was made out for $750,000.

Over the next few months, we developed the website and worked diligently to implement the "leadership pack" plan in the various countries and regions of the world. We would incur a one-time cost for each language translation of the materials of the book, corresponding curriculum, and extra books that would go on the DVD-ROM. Rob hired and led teams of the best translators for the numerous languages. The two generous donations, totaling just over a million dollars, covered the needed capital for our first year.

THE IDEA TO BUILD A TEAM

At this point, let's back up the time line and return to January 2011 and the days immediately following the decision to give away 250,000 books. The two large donations hadn't yet been given, and I'm glad they hadn't because our lack of funds became a catalyst to seek God each morning for a strategy. We needed a plan to communicate the vision, and subsequently build a huge team of men and women who would bring their gift of giving in order to sustain this massive endeavor. This would make it possible for us to resource every pastor and leader, regardless of their language, location, or financial position.

After several mornings of praying, the Holy Spirit whispered to my heart, "Son, you are well-known for your love of golf. Use it to gather. I will draw the right men and women to come join the team and support the mission." My thoughts went immediately to the fact that we have one of the nicest hotels in the nation in Colorado Springs, The Broadmoor, which just so happened to have two championship golf courses. So, I approached Addison and Lisa with the plan.

They listened, and then asked, "When will we do this?"

"Let's do it this summer," I replied.

We were concerned it might not be enough time to pull it off. Would there be sufficient rooms available at the hotel, which just happens to be the longest-standing five-star, five-diamond hotel in the world? It's usually booked out years in advance, and we were targeting the peak season. The other concern: Would our potential guests already have their summer plans in place?

My son took the lead and within a couple of days returned with the news, "Dad, they are booked solid this summer with the exception of one week. We can reserve roughly one hundred rooms, and it just so happens you and Mom are home that week."

"Let's book it!" I said without hesitation.

He cautioned, "We have to sign a contract; we'll be committed. Can we fill the rooms?"

Again, I blurted out, "The rooms will be full." I didn't want to think about it too much; I didn't want to reason myself out of the plan.

I knew there were a lot of churches and businesspeople in the United States who would love to support this endeavor. I called everyone I could think of, and practically everyone was eager to participate. Within a couple of months, we had enough couples to fill the committed rooms.

In planning for the tournament, our team decided not to make this just a golf tournament, but a full-blown event, a memorable experience. We determined that everything would be done with excellence and purpose in order to make the experience especially fun for the spouses who didn't play golf. Lisa would host special gatherings with the women. Upon arrival, we would give beautiful baskets filled with snacks and gifts to each couple. There would be spectacular meals, special experiences unique to The Broadmoor, leadership sessions, and high-quality prizes to all participants—all of this to convey gratitude for joining the team.

Our first Messenger Cup was held in late June 2011. Before the event, I called professional athletes and well-known musicians and asked if they could donate signed items. We also got other businesses to give valuable items or experiences. We auctioned these contributions during the banquet. We raised a little over $340,000 in our first tournament, but it was a bit awkward. We still hadn't connected with the best strategy to share the vision.

That fall, one of our team members had another inspired idea. As we were planning for the second annual tournament in the summer of 2012, he said, "We are auctioning a signed baseball, a football helmet, a signed guitar, and so forth. In auctioning these items, we are not fully funding materials for even one nation. Let's not auction an item—let's auction a nation. The value of a nation is much greater."

We all loved the idea, but it got even better! He continued, "We have highly competitive people coming to this event, so let's create a leaderboard, and as they fund nations, their giving will accumulate on the board, and we will give the balls, guitars, and other prizes to those who have done the most to sponsor nations."

The creative ideas continued flowing. At one point, I protested, "I hate dragging out auctions; a few minutes of silence seem like an eternity. Let's implement a clock, put a small amount of time on the clock, say thirty-five minutes, and tell our participants that once the clock runs out, we will be finished with the auction. Any nation whose project is not funded will be left out. It will create a great sense of urgency."

At this point, let me briefly define a *project*. It involves two things—first, the expense to translate and interpret all the printed, audio, and video components of a leader pack, which costs roughly $17,500 per language. The second is the cost to manufacture and distribute the books or leader packs to a nation. Each country would have anywhere from 500 to 40,000 leaders. Most nations averaged 5,000 to 10,000 leaders, for an average expense of $20,000 to $40,000.

In later meetings, more ideas flowed from the team to enhance the experience, communicate the vision, and pull off the second event.

That year during the auction, we witnessed the pledged funds double from the previous year. With time to spare on the clock, over fifty projects were fully funded. The momentum grew and a year later at the third Messenger Cup, we raised over $1.3 million to fund many more projects.

Every year the cry for resources grew. More nations were sending delegates to Rob, pleading for their people to receive the resources. Eventually, the number of projects passed the 100 mark, and by the sixth Messenger Cup there were over 140 projects and over $2 million raised. In the ninth year, we witnessed almost $3 million come in to fund close to 200 projects!

At the time of this book's release in late 2020, the Messenger Cup team has given over 30 million resources to pastors and leaders in over 100 nations in over 120 languages.

Throughout this time, we were all inspired by one of my heroes, Andrew Carnegie. He is one of history's most well-known philanthropists, giving most of his fortune away. In the value of today's currency, Carnegie gave billions of dollars to charitable works! A good part of this was given to build public libraries. In fact, between the years of 1883 and 1918, he built over 2,500 libraries, most of which are in forty-seven states in the United States.

Let me pose an intriguing question: During what time period did the United States become a world power? It was between 1883 and 1925, the same time frame when Carnegie was building libraries! I believe his making knowledge available to the public contributed to the emergence of America as a world leader.

This principal applies to spiritual knowledge as well! God states:

My people are destroyed for *lack of knowledge*. (Hosea 4:6 NKJV)

My people have gone into captivity, because they have *no knowledge*. (Isaiah 5:13 NKJV)

It's become evident after many years in our ministry that the most effective way to transform a village or town is not to construct a church building. This just keeps the local leadership dependent on us. We are much more effective if we give the indigenous leaders spiritual knowledge that will empower them to influence their village, town, or city. Such knowledge helps produce the faith needed to grow and sustain the work, which, if necessary, will include buildings and other resources.

In the case of our strategic initiative with resources, the amazing reality is that a church building might have cost us tens of thousands of dollars. The leadership pack, which contains hundreds of dollars of resources, only costs us a fraction of that!

The decade of giving leadership packs to the developing church has unquestionably been the most enjoyable of my forty years in ministry. I love being part of a team of men and women united in passion and vision to make disciples of the nations (see Matthew 28:19–20). By uniting, we have far outdone what any of us could have accomplished by ourselves. This effort truly exemplifies the words, "Five of you will chase a hundred, and a hundred of you will chase ten thousand!"

(Leviticus 26:8). (This illustrates another key component of multiplying—uniting together—that we'll cover in a later chapter.)

Our rally cry centers on this parable of Jesus:

> "When you put on a luncheon or a banquet," He said, "don't
> invite your friends, brothers, relatives, and rich neighbors.
> For they will invite you back, and that will be your only
> reward. Instead, invite the poor, the crippled, the lame, and
> the blind. Then at the resurrection of the righteous, God
> will reward you for inviting those who *could not repay* you."
> (Luke 14:12–14)

The leaders we've seeded may not be crippled, lame, or blind, but our tie to this parable is that they *could not repay* us. If I minister for a church or conference in the United States, they say "thank you" by giving Messenger International an honorarium or offering. These leaders in the nations we've invested in can't do this. All team members—marketplace givers, church leaders, and our Messenger staff—realize we have a great privilege: to give without expecting any compensation in return from those we've helped.

A few years ago, Lisa and I traveled to the city of Yerevan, Armenia, where thousands of leaders from all over the Middle East had come for a conference. While there, in a separate auditorium, we gathered the pastors from Iran, Afghanistan, Syria, and similar nations. Cameras were not permitted and identities were kept secret. The presence of God was strong, and I kept thinking, *These leaders should speak to us instead of Lisa and me addressing them.* At one point I stated, "You all see Lisa and me as the heroes. No, it's not John and Lisa Bevere, but rather the businesspeople and churches who have given millions of dollars to bless you with resources. They are the true heroes." At that point, we all broke down and wept.

After the meeting, one Iranian pastor asked, "How can people give such a large amount of money to those they have never met before?"

My reply seemed too simplistic, but it was the truth: "It's the love of God in their hearts." Once again, the tears flowed.

EVEN GREATER MULTIPLICATION

In 2019, we realized our in-house website for distributing the resources had limitations. It had been a good fit for 2011 when we started, but now it was clumsy and limited in its use. For example, the site was way too difficult to navigate on smartphones. Lisa, many of our team members, and I had traveled to many poor and troubled nations. We couldn't help but notice that even though people were living in tents, mud houses, or plywood shacks, the majority had some kind of smartphone. It's actually estimated that as of 2020, over five billion people will have smartphones.

After numerous trips it became apparent that soon, if not already, it would be possible to reach everyone on the planet via online communications. Among others, I felt we were once again experiencing a "Roman Road" moment in history.

Let me briefly explain: Scripture states, "When the right time came, God sent His Son" (Galatians 4:4). The "right time" takes many things into consideration. One important element of the "right time" tells us that the gospel will reach the known world. In 312 BC, the Romans began to develop roadways and shipping routes that covered the known world. By the time Jesus said, "Go into all the world," these routes were well developed. This provided the means to quickly spread the Word of God to the known world.

I believe the right time has again emerged to make way for Jesus's second coming—the internet is the Roman Road of our day. We have the capability of spreading the Word of God to the entire world for the purpose of making disciples of all nations.

Knowing this, our team again began to pray, dream, and strategize. After months of research, we commissioned a project with one of the finest app and web developing companies in the United States. We built a discipleship platform that is high-powered, multifunctional, and user-friendly for iPhone, Android, tablets, and computers. We were determined to build the finest platform possible with today's technology. We wanted church leaders everywhere, but particularly in troubled nations, to have the very best. The remarkable reality is that we've now tracked millions of users from 227 nations and territories who are learning from the books, courses, and other discipleship tools available on the platform. We only have a handful of nations left to reach them all!

After time passed, we thought of additional ways to multiply. In order to expand and strengthen our platform's effectiveness, we decided to bring other notable teachers with unique, transforming messages on the platform as guests. Now leaders all over the world can use their computers, tablets, or phones to train one-on-one or in small groups or churches. Not only has this multiplied the effectiveness of the platform, but it will also long outlive a physical book and will endure for generations to come.*

What if Lisa and I had decided not to write? Or, what if we were content being two best-selling authors and didn't contend for the curricula/studies? What if our team remained satisfied with only reaching individuals and churches in English? What if our staff didn't want to put the energy into gathering a team from all over the United States at The Broadmoor? Each level has presented challenges that have greatly stretched us, forcing us to depend on God's grace. At

---

* To learn more about how you can get involved, visit www.MessengerX.com.

each level, it would have been much easier to coast, and not press on to greater effectiveness in serving others.

When we listen to God's Spirit, we will move step-by-step into greater multiplication. He will not show you every step at the beginning or even two or three steps ahead. It would have been so much easier to look into a crystal ball in my early thirties and see the entire pathway to where we'd be as a team thirty years later. However, if that had been possible, we wouldn't have contended for each step so intensely in prayer and leadership. Also, we would not have acquired the faith and strength of character that occurred with each step of obedience.

It is not mankind's idea to multiply—it is God's idea. Again, it was His first command to mankind, "Any gift I entrust to you is for the purpose of multiplying My kingdom" (my paraphrase of Genesis 1:22 and Matthew 25:14–29). Let me restate this very important point: This multiplication should not put pressure on you because, ultimately, it's His gift. All you have to do is pray, listen, believe, and obey what He puts in your heart.

Bottom line: He will lead you to multiply.

You may be thinking, *My heart is stirred from the testimony you've given in the past three chapters. But I'm a young mother, a student, a professional athlete, an employee—how can I multiply the kingdom?*

This discussion begins in the next chapter.

REFLECT

1. When we look for God's provision or intervention to occur, it often comes in the form of a strategic idea. How have you seen your circumstances change through a God-inspired idea?

2. Receiving wisdom is the most important thing you can do. In what area of your life do you need wisdom? How are you to approach God in order to receive His wisdom?

3. A strategic idea is a gift from God and has the potential to open us to another realm of effectiveness and empower us to multiply. Once an idea is received, what next steps are required of you?

In His grace, God has given us different gifts (charisma) for doing certain things well. So if God has given you the ability to prophesy, speak out with as much faith as God has given you. If your gift is serving others, serve them well. If you are a teacher, teach well. If your gift is to encourage others, be encouraging. If it is giving, give generously. If God has given you leadership ability, take the responsibility seriously. And if you have a gift for showing kindness to others, do it gladly.

—Romans 12:6–8

9

Investing

The apostle Paul highlights various gifts God has given to each of His servants. Again, I don't believe it is an exhaustive list but covers a wide range of divine abilities. You may not agree with me on this, but allow me to share its premise.

I see nowhere on the apostle's list the ability to sing, to argue cases in a court, to surgically remove tumors, to paint inspiring pictures, to play instruments, and many other God-given abilities that we witness on a daily basis. This is why I don't believe it's all-inclusive. If you still disagree, I respect your position; the topic doesn't warrant extended discussion as it isn't a major point.

Returning to the emphasis of Paul's words, I love how the New Living Translation spells out *charisma* as the ability "for doing certain things well." This certainly identifies the main focus of this book. The past three chapters have testified to the multiplication of *prophesying* and *teaching*. Let's turn our attention to a different gift—*giving*.

KINGDOM INVESTING

I have a friend named Mike. He became a believer in Jesus Christ when he was eleven years old; however, he was unproductive in building the kingdom. He grew more and more dissatisfied with this state and, eventually, at the age of thirty-five was fed up with not making an eternal impact. Often those who reach this place immediately attempt to make the change without knowledge, wisdom, and faith. Wisely, Mike approached it differently. He determined that the first step to make a lasting impact was to "fill the tank," so over the next six months he memorized two thousand verses of Scripture!

Soon after this six-month period, he decided to attend a leadership conference in Phoenix, Arizona. He was so poor he couldn't afford a hotel room and had to room with eleven students in a two-bedroom apartment.

A special offering was taken during the conference. The leader encouraged the delegates to pray about what to give. Mike heard the Lord say, "I want you to give $200."

Mike protested, "God, that is all I have!"

The Lord gently replied, "I'm not asking you to give any more."

Mike obeyed and gave all the money he had. God then instructed Mike to give $100 a month above his tithe for the rest of the year.

Soon God started giving him *strategic ideas*, and his new business began to steadily increase. The next year, Mike felt he should give $400 a month above his tithe to build the kingdom.

A year later, the amount went to $1,000 a month above his tithe. The next year, it went to $4,000 per month above his tithe, and the following year it went to $10,000 per month above his tithe.

At this point, Mike asked the Lord for the ability to give $10 million to the kingdom. It seemed like a huge request, almost unattainable, but he was firm in his belief and request. However, what he heard in his heart shocked him: "Son, why are you boxing Me in?" So Mike removed the limits and believed for even more. Soon afterward, his giving started to rapidly escalate, and the next year he gave close to $17,000 per month above his tithe. Then it became $25,000 per month, then $40,000, then $50,000 per month. Eventually, Mike gave

$100,000 per month above his tithe to build the kingdom. The last time I talked with him, he had hit the level of $150,000 per month above his tithe!

Mike has lived very well, but on roughly 10 to 15 percent of his income. Yes, you read that correctly; he gives approximately 85 to 90 percent of what he makes a year. He attributes his success to learning the Bible, listening to God when he prays, and allowing himself to be discipled by those who are more mature than he is.

When it comes to multiplication, you cannot ignore the word *giving*, because it's most often the key ingredient. In the specific area of finances, many well-meaning believers view *offerings* in this light: *What am I willing to give up for the sake of others?* This is noble and godly, but if it's the only perspective, it's incomplete. Allow me to explain.

First, to affirm the positive, God has put His love for people in our heart; this creates an inward desire to unselfishly *give* and *serve*. This should be the preeminent desire in anyone's giving. However, a *wise* giver not only sees an offering as a gift of love and service, but also as an *investment*. To invest is to refrain from consuming a resource in order to grow it. Specifically, in regard to finances, it's to abstain from spending now in order to invest funds for growth.

Lisa and I found two plots of land a few years ago. We felt they were underpriced and would grow in value over time. We possessed the cash to purchase both, and at the time decided to forgo spending the cash for personal consumption in order to make the money grow. The lots did much better than we expected, and our investment doubled in just two years. This resulted in us possessing twice as much cash two years later. We now had the ability to invest at a greater level.

Jesus says that when we invest in the kingdom, we "will be repaid *many times* over in *this* life" (Luke 18:29–30). He did not say "the *next* life" but rather "*this* life." Lisa and I were thrilled to double our investment on the lots, but what Jesus states isn't in the same ball-park; there's a huge difference between *double* and *many times over*. What's the potential of an investment that's multiplied *many times over*? Mike's life is a testimony to this truth.

The apostle Paul compares our giving to planting seeds. While it varies depending on the conditions, on average, one kernel of wheat, if not consumed but rather invested in the soil, will produce over one hundred kernels of wheat. This falls under the category of "many times over." This is why we are told, "Give freely and become more wealthy; be stingy and lose everything" (Proverbs 11:24). When it comes to giv-ing, Solomon, Jesus, and Paul would not have emphasized this truth if believers were to avoid thoughts of increase and multiplication.

Most would view Mike's resolve to live on 10 to 15 percent of his income as solely a sacrifice of love; however, Mike sees the broader picture. Since he is filled with God's wisdom from saturating his soul with two thousand memorized Bible verses, he not only sees it as an act of love, he also sees the investment aspect.

He views it the same way that Lisa and I viewed the two plots of land. He approaches it no differently than a family who owns a successful restaurant. Instead of consuming all the profits personally, the family takes a good percentage of the profits in order to purchase more buildings, hire more personnel, buy more food, and whatever else is required to grow the business. If this is done well, they may eventually have five restaurants, which ultimately would create five times the revenue. The result: They have the ability to be a blessing to many more than if they only owned one restaurant.

If he had considered it as something other than an investment, Mike wouldn't have ascended to understand the more profound meaning of giving. This is exactly what the parable of the talents ad-dresses. Look at Jesus's words: "The servant who received the five bags of silver began to *invest* the money and earned five more" (Matthew

25:16). He specifically uses the word *invest* to illustrate how the servant multiplied.

ANOTHER PARABLE OF MULTIPLICATION

Let's look at a different parable Jesus used to illustrate multiplication:

> The crowd was listening to everything Jesus said. And because
> He was nearing Jerusalem, He told them a story to correct the
> impression that the Kingdom of God would begin right away.
> (Luke 19:11)

I love how this parable is introduced. The people expect Jesus to set up the kingdom and deliver them from the Roman oppression and rule. He adjusts their mentality by giving the accurate perspective— His desire for us to build the kingdom after His departure. But how will this be accomplished? Through *investing*. Listen to the story:

> A nobleman was called away to a distant empire to be crowned
> king and then return. Before he left, he called together ten of
> his servants and divided among them ten pounds of silver, say-
> ing, "*Invest* this for me while I am gone." (Luke 19:12–13)

As in Matthew's story, He instructs us to "invest." We are not to be lazy with what we've been entrusted with, but we are to work *hard* and *smart*.

Even though these two parables seem the same, they're different. Let's examine what sets them apart. First, Matthew speaks of three servants, whereas Luke identifies ten servants. Second, in Matthew's story, each servant is given different amounts, but in this one each is given an equal amount—one pound of silver. Third, in Matthew's story, a portion was not just one pound but a bag containing seventy-five pounds of silver. In comparing the two stories, I believe Matthew's story speaks of gifts, which are not distributed evenly, whereas Luke's story portrays what every believer is equally given by God—foundational faith, the love of God, the Word of God, our covenant blessings, and so forth. However, the underlying principles are the same. Let's continue the story:

> After he was crowned king, he returned and called in the servants to whom he had given the money. He wanted to find out what their profits were. The first servant reported, "Master, I *invested* your money and made *ten times* the original amount!"
>
> "Well done!" the king exclaimed. "You are a good servant. You have been *faithful* with the little I entrusted to you, so you will be governor of *ten cities* as your reward." (Luke 19:15–17)

There are several points to highlight. First, the servant invested what was given to him. Second, he worked *hard* and *smart*, which resulted in tenfold multiplication. To work *smart* is to be in tune with the wisdom of God, and this only occurs by listening to God's counsel, as my friend Mike did. Third, once again *multiplication* is directly attributed to *faithfulness*. There is no other action or virtue mentioned, because in God's eyes, to be faithful is to multiply. Finally, the servant's eternal reward is proportional to his multiplication—this first servant is entrusted with ten cities to govern.

Now let's look at the second servant:

> The next servant reported, "Master, I invested your money and made five times the original amount."

"Well done!" the king said. "You will be governor over five cities." (Luke 19:18–19)

This one didn't multiply ten times, but five times. His eternal reward reflected his level of investing—five cities, not ten. Why didn't he multiply ten times as the other servant? Did he not listen as closely to God's wisdom? Did he miss opportunities? Did he coast in his later years, as Stan from our first chapter was planning to do? Did he have a retirement mentality?

I spoke on multiplication in a leadership conference a few years back. One of California's top commercial property developers, who had already given millions to the kingdom, came up to me after I spoke. He looked to be in a state of shock but also enlightened. He said, "John, I've slipped into a mentality of coasting because of how successful I've been. It's an easy attitude to fall into, but now I see the error. Moving forward, I will be more focused and diligent to multiply what God has given me." It's possible that his genuine repentance will alter his course from being a five-time multiplier to a ten-time multiplier.

How about the third servant?

But the third servant brought back only the original amount of money and said, "Master, I hid your money and kept it safe. I was afraid because you are a hard man to deal with, taking what isn't yours and harvesting crops you didn't plant."

"You wicked servant!" the king roared. "Your own words condemn you. If you knew that I'm a hard man who takes what isn't mine and harvests crops I didn't plant, why didn't you deposit my money in the bank? At least I could have gotten some interest on it." (Luke 19:20–23)

As in the story from Matthew, this servant had the same two major flaws. First, he was afraid and, second, he didn't know the character of his master. This story once again signifies that *maintaining* what God gives us isn't *faithfulness*, rather *wickedness*. Notice the king *roared*! The lazy attitude angered the ruler and he showed it! Very sobering when you think about it.

What happens next only strengthens what we concluded from Matthew's account:

> Then, turning to the others standing nearby, the king ordered, "Take the money from this servant, and give it to the one who has ten pounds."
>
> "But, master," they said, "he already has ten pounds!"
>
> "Yes," the king replied, "and to those who use well what they are given, even more will be given. But from those who do nothing, even what little they have will be taken away." (Luke 19:24–26)

Once again, we see that God is not a socialistic Creator but is more "capitalistic" in His thinking. Jesus pointedly illustrates that the bystanders protested because the first servant already had ten pounds of silver, and the master corrected their "let's be fair" mentality by declaring, "To those who *invest* well, more will be given." And conversely, "Those who *maintain*, even what little they have will be taken away."

It is both an amazing and scary reality that if we don't do what Mike did, spend an abundant amount of time in God's Word and in communion with Him, we can easily filter God's character through the environment we live in. It may be society's filter, Hollywood's filter, Instagram's filter, a news network's filter, a filter of a harsh father, a religious filter, or any other life experience or sociological mindset filter we either like or dislike. When we know God and His Word intimately, we can recognize these faulty filters.

ALL ARE CALLED TO GIVE

Mike has the *gift* of *giving*; he excels in it. However, all of us should be *givers*.

To help clarify, let me compare this to Jesus's commission to go into all the world and preach the gospel (see Mark 16:15–16). This charge is given to every believer. All of us should be ambassadors and share the gospel with those who are lost. This is also captured in Paul's words: "Do the work of an evangelist" (2 Timothy 4:5 NKJV), which are directed to all believers.

But there is a unique office and complementary gifting called *evangelist*. Paul writes, "And He Himself gave . . . *some evangelists*" (Ephesians 4:11 NKJV). Not all, but some, are called to stand in this office. This gift excels in the ability to bring in a harvest of souls. In the book of Acts, Philip—not all believers—is called an evangelist (see Acts 21:8). Billy Graham, T.L. Osborn, and Reinhard Bonnke were all gifted evangelists. They, with the help of their teams, each won tens of millions of souls. They multiplied their God-given gift, no differently than did Mike and the others I referred to earlier.

Just as they were, we are all called to *give*, but there are some who have the *charisma* of *giving*. They excel in financial giving just as the evangelist excels in soul winning. The message of this book focuses on multiplying our God-given gifts. However, since financial giving is such a crucial aspect of multiplication, for the rest of this chapter I want to zero in on what each of us are called to do—multiply in the area of financial giving.

In my forty years of ministry, I've witnessed two extremes when it comes to finances and giving. These extremes affect far too many in the church, and it is my sincere hope that this will change. First, there are those who give only to get; they want more for selfish reasons. If we are objective and call it out for what it is, a word to identify this motivation is *covetousness*.

Sadly, this errant mentality has helped birth the other extreme (the old pendulum swing). It occurs mostly with people who don't study the overall counsel of God's Word, the way Mike did. They despise any teaching that would build people's faith toward financial giving. This attitude can even go to the extreme of resenting anything to do with offerings. In essence, advocates of this idea hinder their own effectiveness, as well as that of those who listen to them. The result is that the overall work of the gospel is restrained.

After coming to Jesus, Lisa and I were members of a church that taught extensively on giving. It was the 1980s and during that time, many were more self-focused than missional focused. Even though our church's teaching was mostly accurate, due to a lack of character, many people gave out of motives to receive bigger homes, better luxury cars, expensive vacations, and various other narcissistic "wants." The focus was no different than what many unbelievers pursue, except that it had a scriptural formula. Lisa and I knew from the start that something was out of balance, but we couldn't articulate just what it was.

Honestly, after being in this environment, it took some purging and maturing for Lisa and me to see giving in a wholesome light. The church's leader eventually succumbed to temptation and lost everything. After seeing the outcome, it was tempting for us to swing the pendulum, but we were committed to believing the Word of God over experiences.

One eye-opening encounter happened a couple of years after we were sent out by this church into our own ministry. I was in a service getting ready to preach when the Holy Spirit asked me, "Son, do you know what a *religious spirit* is?"

I'd read, spoken, heard others speak on, and even written about what a religious mindset is, but when He asked, I immediately realized there was something I didn't comprehend. I replied, "I must not know. Otherwise You wouldn't ask me. So, what is it?"

I heard the Holy Spirit answer, "A religious spirit is one who uses My Word to execute his own will. This person doesn't carry out My instructions with My heart's desires being preeminent. He applies My Word for his own gain."

These words were catalytic to the needed adjustments in my heart from the toxic environment I'd been in. This message from the Holy Spirit revealed that we can give and even reap the benefits, but it can be done with wrong intentions. God's laws will be beneficial, even if the motive isn't correct.

Since the apostle Paul used farming in regard to giving, allow me to do the same. A farmer can plant seeds for one purpose: to hoard all his crops. Any food he can't consume, he builds bigger silos to contain it, and he says within himself, "You have enough stored away for years to come. Now take it easy! Eat, drink, and be merry!" (Luke 12:19).

God's response to him is, "You fool!" (verse 20). The principle of sowing and harvesting worked for this farmer, even though as Jesus points out, he was covetous.

On the other hand, a different farmer may desire to help and feed people. He will experience the same harvest as the first farmer, but his response is different. He says within himself, "Wow, not only will I eat, but now I can help my community be stronger and healthier! I can be generous!"

The law of sowing and harvesting works equally for both men. It would be ridiculous for everyone to stop planting and harvesting for the motive of the first man's covetousness. Yet, this is what many have done in the area of giving into the kingdom.

Let's dive deeply into Paul's words. He begins by saying:

> I thought I should send these brothers ahead of me to make
> sure *the gift* you promised is ready. But I want it to be a willing
> *gift*, not one given grudgingly. (2 Corinthians 9:5)

There is no doubt, Paul is speaking of a financial gift or an offering. He continues to use the principle of farming to illustrate what God would do for those who give:

> Remember this—a farmer who plants only a few seeds will get
> a small crop. But the one who plants generously will get a generous crop. (2 Corinthians 9:6)

If our sole motive in giving is to help people, then why does Paul talk about the harvest we will receive from giving? Is it wrong to have a secondary desire of multiplication, especially when it will help fuel and increase the primary desire to build lives for the kingdom? Could it be Paul is training new believers in the Corinthian church how to multiply their effectiveness, as Jesus did in the parable of the talents? Is Paul appealing to them to be moved with compassion, but at the same time to also invest for the purpose of being a greater blessing? I do think this is Paul's motive, for look how he continues:

> You must each decide in your heart how much to give. And don't
> give reluctantly or in response to pressure. "For God loves a
> person who gives cheerfully." And God will generously provide
> all you need. Then you will always have *everything you need* and
> *plenty left over to share with others*. (2 Corinthians 9:7–8)

Notice two things will be accomplished. Personal needs will be met, but also Paul specifically states that there will be *plenty left over to share with others*. Our capacity to be generous is multiplied, because we have invested or planted seed. This motive is reinforced even more:

> For God is the one who provides seed for the farmer and then bread to eat. In the same way, He will provide and *increase your resources* and then produce a great harvest of *generosity* in you. Yes, you will be enriched in every way so that you can *always be generous*. (2 Corinthians 9:10–11)

Paul specifically states that through giving, God will *increase your resources*. This will give you the ability to *always be generous*. This truth is not only for those endowed with the gift of financial giving, but pertains to every believer. It's a spiritual law that God put in place long ago.

When Lisa and I started in ministry, our income was $18,000 per year. We could barely pay our bills. I remember our first Christmas in ministry. We had to take our spare few dollars and buy supplies to assemble small baskets of homemade gifts. We didn't have enough money to purchase anything else.

A couple of years later, our pastor took a special offering. Lisa and I wanted to be a part of the outreach. God spoke to us: "Give $1,000."

In the two years prior to this, we had saved and saved so that we could make a down payment on a small house. We had accumulated $1,800; it was all we owned, we had no retirement, investments, or other savings to fall back on. If we gave this amount, we would only have $800 left to our name. It appeared that our years of savings would be significantly diminished by this one offering. Seemingly, it would be years before we'd have enough money for a house down payment. However, we gave because we wanted to be a part of impacting others. We also wanted to be more generous. We knew from Scripture, the only way we could increase our capacity to give was by multiplying the little we had.

As the years have passed, we've been able to give more than baskets, and more than a $1,000 offering. Just this year alone, we've been able to give to missions fifty times that first big offering. We want to impact more lives in every way. God multiplied our ability and empowered us to be generous. The Passion Translation brings this truth out beautifully:

This generous God who supplies abundant seed for the farmer, which becomes bread for our meals, is even more extravagant toward you. First He supplies every need, plus more. Then He *multiplies* the seed as you sow it, so that *the harvest of your generosity will grow*. You will be abundantly enriched in every way as you give generously on every occasion. (2 Corinthians 9:10–11 TPT)

Notice He is extravagant toward us. For a purpose, He will *multiply* the investment we make in building the kingdom, so that our *generosity will grow*. We build up our heavenly accounts, where moths and rust do not corrupt, nor do thieves break in and steal, and we will also draw from the accounts in this life. Yes, there is an eternal reward, but there is an account we develop for generosity in this age too. Paul made this very clear when he wrote to the Philippian believers:

Not that I seek or am eager for [your] gift, but I do seek and am eager for the fruit which increases to your credit [the harvest of blessing that is accumulating to your account]. (Philippians 4:17 AMPC)

Just as some people have bank accounts, stock accounts, and investment accounts, all believers have a heavenly account. That account empowers us to multiply our effectiveness in building the kingdom on this earth. What would happen if all believers came to know, understand, and believe in this spiritual law? We would reach the world so much faster with the gospel! Is it clear why the enemy of the kingdom would attempt in every way to keep believers from sowing financial seeds?

Lisa and I are close friends with a husband and wife named Phil and Dana who are outrageous givers. They give to the kingdom approximately 50 percent of their income. Just recently, they gave a ministry a $100,000 gift for an outreach. Two days later, they gave another ministry $100,000 for a different mission's outreach. I know this because Messenger International was the second ministry.

Phil started his business years ago and it performed in an average manner—far from superior. However, twenty-five years ago, Phil and Dana made a commitment to God that they would give $250,000 to a ministry over the following three years. It seemed utterly impossible, but they wanted to make room for God's intervention.

Phil's business blossomed, but he was unaware of just how well things were going. Three months later, he realized there was an extra $250,000 in the account. So, he and Dana decided to give the pledge immediately, rather than spreading it out over three years. He told me, "John, that's when the ridiculous levels of giving started for us."

Similar to Mike, they refrained from drawing back. They pressed on when it would have been easy to draw back; consequently, their heavenly account was enlarged to measures they'd never dreamed possible. Isn't this available to you and me? Paul emphatically tells us:

Never doubt God's mighty power to work in you and accomplish all this. He will achieve infinitely more than your greatest request, your most unbelievable dream, and exceed your wildest imagination! He will outdo them all, for His miraculous power constantly energizes you. (Ephesians 3:20 TPT)

BREAKTHROUGH

I've learned through years of ministry that we will be tested in both our *charisma* and *financial giving*. There may be a season in which no publisher is interested in talking with you about your book; in fact, that season may last years. You consider stopping because it's been a lot of hard work, the book seems to be going nowhere, and you see no possible way of changing it. But you continue in obedience. Suddenly the *breakthrough* comes.

Or you give and give but are not seeing quick harvests, and it seems like your finances are too tight to do any more. But then God speaks to you, as with Mike, and you obey even when it seems impossible. You witness a *breakthrough* and enter another realm of giving.

What is a *breakthrough*? Dictionary.com defines it as "an act or instance of removing or surpassing an obstruction or restriction."[12] Picture this: Water is restricted by a wall. The water continues to rise, but the wall remains an obstruction. All of a sudden, cracks begin to appear in the wall; a short time later, water suddenly bursts through. Now the obstruction is eliminated, and water flows freely where it was previously restrained. That is a breakthrough.

King David declares, "God has broken through my enemies *by my hand* like a breakthrough of water" (1 Chronicles 14:11 NKJV). The water rising is a picture of our continual obedience to truth and after the breakthrough, the free-flowing water represents fruitfulness or abundance.

In regard to our friends Phil and Dana, after they gave the first $100,000 gift, Phil told me that their business had a record week and earned back the whole $100,000—and more—in just that week. This is what a breakthrough looks like. It didn't start out this way for them; they gave and gave and didn't immediately see much of a harvest. But after years and years of sowing continually, they experienced a breakthrough and the harvests almost seem to come as quickly as the planting.

It is a fulfillment of the prophet Amos's words: "'The time will come,' says the LORD, 'when the grain and grapes will grow faster than they can be harvested'" (Amos 9:13). In the New King James Version, the truth is brought out in a beautiful picture:

"Behold, the days are coming," says the LORD,
"When the plowman shall overtake the reaper,
And the treader of grapes him who sows seed;
The mountains shall drip with sweet wine,
And all the hills *shall flow with it.*

The harvester will have such an abundant harvest that the planter will overtake him.

Those who tread grapes will still be stomping on the previous season's grapes while the plowmen begin their work for the following year! But the picture of the result is remarkable. The plowmen, harvesters, and those who stomp on the grapes all have the common desire to make wine. Listen to the declared outcome: "There shall be a continual flow of wine; it shall not stop, no more unfruitful times" (author's paraphrase).

There is a place in regard to our *charisma* and *financial giving* in which this very thing happens. It happened with Mike, as well as with Phil and Dana. In regard to Messenger International, we have numerous testimonies of lives changed by the resources we've sown throughout the years. The grapes are growing faster than they can be harvested!

Many quit just short of the breakthrough. They've been overwhelmed by adversity or the lack of desired results. Lisa and I could have easily turned to reason and logic and ignored the voice of the

Spirit of God. We needed at least $5,000 for a down payment on a much-needed house. Most nice apartments in our city were adult-only communities, and babies were not permitted. We could have reasoned, "Let's first get into a house, and then we can save and give $1,000 on a future outreach." We would have missed a prime opportunity to invest in the kingdom and grow our resources.

The amazing aspect of the story is that six months later, we miraculously had the $5,000. Lisa received a sum of money from an account we were unaware of that her father had set up. Additionally, two individuals, without knowing our need, gave us $2,000. We were in our new house less than a year later. It was miraculous, and much better for our faith and endurance to see Him provide when it seemed "impossible." I don't believe this would have happened had we hung on to the $1,000 the Holy Spirit instructed us to give.

At this point on this topic, it's wise to give a warning: We shouldn't operate presumptuously. What do I mean? We should seek the counsel of our senior Partner, the Holy Spirit. He tells us, "I *am* the LORD your God, Who teaches you to profit, Who leads you by the way you should go" (Isaiah 48:17 NKJV). Maintaining a sensitive conscience (the place where the Holy Spirit enlightens us) and obedience to what He shows us is paramount, because He is the one who leads us to profit in our kingdom investments. We would not have given the $1,000 had He not whispered the request to our hearts.

Some people don't listen to His counsel. Others can't hear His counsel, because they have said "no" too many times. Their conscience is no longer tender. If that's you, simply repent and ask His forgiveness for suppressing His voice. Your sensitivity will immediately return; He is quick to forgive! But then listen to His promptings, and don't let the voice of reason talk you out of it.

REFLECT

1. God has put His love for people in your heart, which should position you to *give* and *serve*. In what ways at present do you serve and give to others? What are some creative ways you can grow in the areas of giving and serving?

2. A wise giver sees an offering not only as a gift of love and service, but also as an *investment*. Through your giving and serving, what type of return on your investment can you expect? How does your attitude toward serving and giving change when they're viewed as an investment?

3. You will be tested in both your *charisma* and *financial giving*. During these tests, you'll experience moments when your harvest will seem delayed and your labor unproductive. When you're tempted to give up, what should your response be? How do you keep yourself encouraged?

God has given each of you a gift from

His great variety of spiritual gifts.

Use them well to serve one another.

—1 Peter 4:10

10

The Catalyst

In this pivotal chapter, I'll unpack the *catalyst* of *effective increase*. In using the word *effective*, I'm speaking of multiplication that endures forever.

A *catalyst* is a key ingredient precipitating or accelerating an event or change (my definition taken from many dictionaries). We are all given gifts, but what triggers their enduring potential is found in the apostle Peter's words, "Use them well to *serve*." Serving is the *catalyst*, but genuine serving is always motivated by love. The apostle Paul writes:

> For we remember before our God and Father how you put
> faith into practice, how your *love motivates you to serve others*.
> (1 Thessalonians 1:3 TPT)

True serving originates out of a heart burning with love. It's an inner disposition that is not altered by adversity, hardship, or any other unfavorable circumstances. It manifests sometimes in word, but most often, in action.

TURKEY LADY

I'll illustrate serving with a story. The couple I'm highlighting are very close friends who have asked to remain anonymous in their mission. So, in keeping with their desire, I'll use fictional names.

Riley and Dave live in a suburb of one of the largest cities in the United States. It was destiny for them to meet, as their apartments were right next to each other.

Soon after getting married, Riley wondered why most churches, homeless shelters, and other charity organizations provide meals and gifts at Christmas, but little is done for the holiday of Thanksgiving. She believes Thanksgiving is important because it focuses on family and centers on a meal. Many single moms, the disabled, and the homeless struggle to provide or participate in a suitable meal. She believes soup kitchens serve a needed purpose but lack the intimacy a home-cooked meal can provide for a family.

Riley has stated, "On our own, each of us has the opportunity to make an impact, but together the impact is greater." She's well versed in Scripture and knows that the efforts of two working together in harmony are tenfold of what they can accomplish alone (see Deuteronomy 32:30). She's also well aware of the fact that results keep escalating as more believers unite. Another truth burning in her heart is that true servants want to be a part of a team and don't care if they get the credit. Riley's attitude personifies these important ingredients for multiplication.

For her first Thanksgiving opportunity, Riley collected money from family and friends to purchase turkeys. With a multiplying mindset, she and Dave promised to match dollar for dollar all that was received. That year, she bought eleven turkeys and delivered them anonymously from the trunk of her car. The second year, the number rose to thirty-one turkeys.

The third year, she told her family and friends that they could share the vision with other friends, as long as they kept it anonymous. They did, and the effort started to rapidly multiply. By the fifth year, they had touched five hundred families and were able to add two cans of vegetables and stuffing to each donation.

It was at this point that she formally set up an *anonymous* distribution agreement with the Salvation Army. This charity organization is connected to social services and was able to set up an application process to screen for the truly needy. The people chosen had no other options for provision (food stamps, government programs, etc.). Riley and her team set up a drive-through and a walk-up distribution site on the grounds of the Salvation Army.

There were many who improvised in order to receive their needed food. They pulled wagons, rode bikes, pushed baskets, asked neighbors for rides, or just walked up and carried away the turkey, vegetables, and stuffing—sometimes for long distances—back to their trailer, apartment, park, or other place outdoors where they lived. One homeless man had figured out how to cook the turkey outside for himself and his homeless friends using a discarded fryer and propane tank.

Eventually, the distribution became so large that a new site was needed to facilitate the volume of people. A neighboring YMCA had a large vacant lot, but relations were strained between the Y and the Salvation Army. The need prompted the two organizations to confront their differences. They reconciled and have since worked together with Riley's project, as well as other community efforts.

Each year, Riley and Dave set a goal to beat the previous year's distribution. They determined that no person in their entire area would go without a proper Thanksgiving meal. As the number grew, the distribution became more complex and difficult, especially with increased prices and some friends dropping out or moving. The couple was stronger financially and didn't want progress stalled at this time, so they decided to match every dollar donated with two dollars. (As a side note, it's no wonder their financial strength increased in those six years. God was multiplying their giving so they could be more effective.)

In Riley's words, "Somehow, some way, God would always supply money from different sources, causing the totals to climb higher
and higher." And what makes it more amazing is that the couple determined from the beginning that they would not receive one penny
from government programs or any corporations. It all had to come
from family, friends, and friends of friends.

As the numbers escalated, new challenges arose. It became impossible to dispense all the turkeys in one day, as the volume of people
was so large. Riley and Dave were forced to add a second distribution
day, but this created a significant obstacle: Where would they store
the turkeys overnight for the second day's distribution? Riley was persistent in her search for an answer. At the midnight hour, a major
grocery store chain where they bought all the turkeys stepped up and
donated the use of refrigerated trucks. Now the money could be spent
on food rather than storage.

There were numerous other hurdles and struggles to overcome,
too many to list. This couple's faith is strong and their resolve is ad-
amant. In the face of adversity, they continually prayed, cried out to
God, came up with inspired strategic ideas, and found favor with people who could help.

They've just hit their twenty-sixth year of serving, and as I'm
writing this, this year alone they have fed 10,500 families (if there
is an average of four per family, that would be 42,000 people). They
have effectively fed every needy person in their entire county, and
a good portion of the two neighboring counties (keep in mind this
area includes one of the largest cities in the United States). In doing
so, they filled five tractor trailers (each forty-eight feet long) with
turkeys and three tractor trailers with vegetables and stuffing. Over
two hundred volunteers are mobilized, with many of them working
tirelessly over a span of several days. Many of them have been with

Riley from the beginning. Here's what's amazing: Most of the volunteers still don't know the identity of the "Turkey Lady"!

It would be impossible to list the miracles, stories, and testimonies of lives changed by their multiplication. Numerous people have come to know Jesus, including Riley's husband, Dave, and many have returned to faith. Families have reconciled, and many people have been inspired—including government workers, grocery store employees, Salvation Army and YMCA employees, volunteers and, in some ways, the entire community.

Allow me to share several short stories. One of Riley's friends is the treasurer of a local motorcycle club. Every year, he asks them to take up a collection for the Turkey Lady. They actually challenge each other to see who can give the most. Last year she got a text after Thanksgiving that the bikers were increasing their donation by $3,000 more for next Thanksgiving.

One year, the Turkey Lady team decided to donate the overage to a local church. It inspired the church to use Riley's model to start their own program of helping the poor during Thanksgiving and other times of the year.

Salvation Army team members that have been transferred to different states are eager to start programs patterned after Riley's. Others have moved into her area and couldn't wait to learn about the ministry, as they'd heard Riley's story from afar through the ranks of the Salvation Army.

Riley is not a pastor, she doesn't work for a church, and she is not a business or corporate woman. She is a wife, mom, and devoted believer who faithfully attends church. She is well aware of the fact that she serves a mighty God who delights in her multiplication. I'm honored to be this couple's friend.

THE NUMBER ONE EXAMPLE
OF ETERNAL MULTIPLICATION

Serving motivated by love is the catalyst for multiplication. Consider some of the great stories of multiplication in Scripture. Of course, the one that tops them all is Jesus. He says:

> If you want to be the greatest one, then live as one called to serve others. The path to promotion and prominence comes by having the heart of a bond-slave who serves everyone. For even the Son of Man did not come expecting to be served by everyone, but *to serve everyone*, and to give His life as the ransom price in exchange for the salvation of many. (Mark 10:43–45 TPT)

Jesus identifies the path to true greatness—seeking to serve, not to be served. It's no surprise He identifies His supreme act of serving with these words: "I tell you the truth, unless a kernel of wheat is planted in the soil and dies, it remains alone. But its death will produce many new kernels" (John 12:24). Once again, we hear of *planting* (or *investing*) and *harvesting*. Just as one *invested* wheat kernel yields a multitude of kernels, Jesus's obedience to serve produced multitudes of sons and daughters of God. What an example! He paved the way and set the bar, showing us how to *effectively* multiply. Jesus says to us:

> You call me "Teacher" and "Lord," and you are right, because that's what I am. And since I, your Lord and Teacher, have washed your feet, you ought to wash each other's feet. I have *given you an example to follow*. Do as I have done to you. (John 13:13–15)

As a leader and communicator, I know the importance of the *final word*. This is the statement or message you leave with your reader, listener, student, team member, employee, child, or anyone else. It's the prevailing thought you want your hearers to have as they move forward.

In His time on earth, what was the final word from Jesus? Interestingly, it was an illustrated sermon He gave before His crucifixion— the washing of His followers' feet.

I'm going to be honest with you; as a young believer I intensely disliked any time someone suggested in a small group, "Let's wash each other's feet." I'd immediately think of a trivial reason to suddenly slip out, because I just didn't like men touching my feet!

Years later, I'm relieved to know the foot washing was more of a tradition that my friends were holding on to. A parallel example is when Moses put the serpent on the pole (see Numbers 21:8–9), and all who looked upon it were healed of snake bites. It was miraculous and powerful. However, many generations later, Israel made an idol of this very serpent (see 2 Kings 18:4). They highlighted the object instead of understanding that originally, years earlier, the focus was obedience to the Lord's instruction.

In the 1980s, we followed a similar path in my Bible study groups. We got the "foot washing" thing out of whack. We focused more on the action, rather than what it represented. Back in the first century, the roads weren't paved, animals were the only mode of transportation other than walking, and there were no Adidas or Nike tennis shoes. People wore sandals or, in many cases, no shoes at all, so their feet were exposed to an abundance of dirt, animal feces, and other grime. It's safe to say that in that environment, stinky, dirty feet reached a level unknown to our Western world today.

When people entered a wealthy person's house, servants or slaves were required to clean the feet of their master, his family, and the guests. In a typical upper-class home, there were a variety of responsibilities: stables to be managed, food to be prepared, rooms to be cleaned, among others. The assignment of washing feet was reserved for the lowliest servant. In some circles, the designation went even further; this nasty task was exclusively assigned to the lowest female servants, as they were considered the only ones "unworthy" enough to do something so disgusting.

For the last supper, the twelve disciples were in such a house, one large enough to host Jesus's entire team in a separate room. It possibly was the most affluent home in the city. Hours earlier, each of these twelve men had had their feet washed by the lowest servant. But, shockingly, the same evening, Jesus not only grabbed the basin and pitcher of water, but He also disrobed—removing the symbol of His position as Teacher, and began to wash their feet. They knew exactly what was going on and what it represented. In contrast, in college, I was confused and even repulsed by the practice because my feet were clean; I had just taken a shower before the Bible study. It also unsettled me. *Why is some guy I barely know attempting to wash my feet?*

If you reread Jesus's words, they'll take on a much greater meaning. He was making a lasting impression; one that would stay with these disciples for the rest of their lives. A *final word.*

In a nutshell, in order to be great, we are to voluntarily take the place of the lowliest servant. Could this be why Jesus says, "I am gentle and lowly in heart" (Matthew 11:29 ESV)?

It took a while to really grasp this. In my early days as a believer, it seemed many of us viewed ministry as just the opposite. Our unspoken belief was, *"Significance isn't attained until you are speaking to or leading many."* Serving was for people in the lower positions of our church. If you worked hard enough, eventually you would be a person of importance. Oh, how messed up our perception was!

I'm so grateful for the Holy Spirit's patience in the maturing process! He transformed my thinking, but it took time. As stated earlier, my first four years of ministry mostly involved taking care of our pastor's personal needs.

One day while I was running an errand, God's Spirit whispered, "Son, if I promote you, it will be a *greater position of serving*. If you mess up now, it's just a dry-cleaned shirt. In public ministry it won't be a replaceable shirt; rather, it will be lives, the people I love damaged." I was riveted by His words. Not only did He communicate that higher positions would include greater serving responsibilities, but He also communicated the importance of always being faithful in the smaller matters. My level of serving wouldn't change with the true riches: people.

Rebekah

One riveting example of multiplication from selfless serving in the Old Testament is seen in Rebekah. Let's briefly review the story.

Abraham sent his most trusted servant back to the country he'd left to find a wife for his heir, Isaac. The servant left promptly, taking ten camels for the long journey.

Upon arrival, Abraham's servant realized it was the time of day that young women came to the community well for water. He prayed, "This is my request. I will ask one of them, 'Please give me a drink from your jug.' If she says, 'Yes, have a drink, and I will water your camels, too!'—let her be the one you have selected as Isaac's wife" (Genesis 24:14).

Before he was finished praying, Rebekah approached with her water jug, so he asked her for a drink. What happens next is spectacular:

"Yes, my lord," she answered, "have a drink." And she *quickly*
lowered her jug from her shoulder and gave him a drink.
When she had given him a drink, she said, "I'll draw water for

your camels, too, until they have had enough to drink." So she
quickly emptied her jug into the watering trough and *ran back*
to the well to draw water for all his camels. (Genesis 24:18–20)

The servant watched her in silence until she had given all ten
camels sufficient water. In these few verses we find many remarkable
traits involved in Rebekah's serving. I'll list them one by one:

- *Eager.* She didn't drag her feet. She did everything swiftly, even
  running back and forth to the well. Slow or convenient serving is not true serving. Have you ever noticed people serving,
  but they do so lethargically with an attitude of "I'm tired from
  all this work"? That's not Rebekah or any true servant. True
  servants have a willing and energetic attitude, which is evident
  from their actions.

- *Extra Mile.* Servants excel. Rebekah far surpassed what was
  asked. Since most of us have not owned camels or lived in a
  Middle Eastern desert, we wouldn't pick up on this factor that
  makes Rebekah's service even more stunning. After a long
  trip, a typical thirsty camel can drink thirty to fifty gallons of
  water. Abraham's servant had ten camels! Let's do the math:
  If each camel drank just thirty gallons, that means Rebekah
  had to carry three hundred gallons of water from the well! If
  a typical jug contained five gallons (forty pounds), she had to
  make sixty trips back and forth from the well.

  But it's even more amazing! There were two types of wells
  in those days. One allowed that a rope be tied to the jug and
  lowered from the surface to the water level in the pit. The
  other required going down twenty to thirty steps to the water
  level. Do we know which kind of well Rebekah was using? We
  sure do—the second one, because later when the servant related Rebekah's actions to her family, he said, "She *went down*

to the spring and drew water" (verse 45). Not only did she make sixty trips with five gallons of water on her shoulders, but she did it while navigating all those steps on each trip. And keep in mind—she volunteered to do this without being asked! Which brings us to the next point.

- *Responsive.* A true servant doesn't wait to be asked when a need is evident; he or she moves forward immediately. In all my years of experience, it's become quite evident that when people consistently wait to be told, they don't multiply. Those who are always the first to go into action are the ones who increase.

- *Committed.* Even though the task was difficult, Rebekah was diligent in serving. Through the years I've observed a pattern: the harder the task, the more quickly great attitudes diminish—it's human nature. However, we have the nature of Jesus Christ. He never quit, even when He went through unimaginable resistance and hardship. Live from the nature of Jesus and be inspired by Rebekah!

- *Completion.* Rebekah didn't stop until the work was finished. She was not a quitter. Doing ninety-nine percent of a task is not finishing a task. We recall how King Saul did this in the battle of the Amalekites: When he killed tens of thousands of people, but spared one, God did not reward His efforts (see 1 Samuel 15). Rebekah did all that she did not knowing there was a reward for her labor. This is the true sign of servanthood: Servants don't labor for the purpose of the reward, but they see the act of serving as its own reward. They love the joy, sense of fulfillment, and satisfaction that serving provides. If there is a reward, it's just an added blessing, not the motivation. The reward for Rebekah was magnificent. She didn't realize that the ten camels all bore treasures and gifts for her, and that she would be married to a godly man. But neither of these was the significant prize: The enduring reward was that she entered into God's promise to Abraham. She would be the mother of many nations. All nations would be blessed through her. Rebekah multiplied significantly.

OTHER EXAMPLES

There are many other scriptural examples of eternal multiplication resulting from a heart to serve. Here are a few more you can investigate in detail during your personal study time.

Ruth

Similar to Rebekah, the Moabite Ruth was encouraged three times by her mother-in-law, Naomi, to return to her homeland. But Ruth refused, saying:

> Don't ask me to leave you and turn back. Wherever you go,
> I will go; wherever you live, I will live. Your people will be
> my people, and your God will be my God. (Ruth 1:16)

Ruth, much like Rebekah, was willing to go the extra mile, work hard, and stay committed, even when the going got rough. Ruth's road probably was more difficult than Rebekah's. Since she was a Moabite, she was most likely persecuted by the town's citizens for her race and where she came from. Yet she endured any hardship to faithfully serve her mother-in-law.

What was the result? She became an ancestor of many notables, including King David, King Solomon, and all the kings of Judah. Most importantly, she was in the lineage of Jesus. She too entered into the covenant of eternal multiplication promised to Abraham.

Elisha

Elisha determined to stay with and serve Elijah, even when Elijah encouraged him three times to leave. Even when the other prophets, more than once, mocked and sneered that he was wasting his time serving Elijah, Elisha stayed. The analysis of the others seemed logical—they'd become full-time prophets, gaining status and experience. What would be Elisha's lot when Elijah was taken? Had he wasted his years serving Elijah without any opportunities to build his own ministry? That was the logic of the other prophets, but Elisha didn't listen. Instead, rather firmly, he told them each time to "be quiet!" (see 2 Kings 2). He would not be deterred from serving and completed his assignment.

Elisha's demeanor was similar to that of Rebekah and Ruth. What was the outcome? He ended up doing twice as many miracles as Elijah and was able to do what Elijah didn't—put an end to Jezebel's dynasty. He multiplied!

Gehazi

Gehazi had the chance to multiply Elisha's work, but he didn't have the heart of a servant. He was self-seeking and covetous, so he didn't effectively multiply (see 2 Kings 5).

X

In the New Testament we see men who served widows' tables. They took the responsibility seriously. Hands were laid on them to ensure that the task was done well. The result was impressive, for in the book of Acts we read this astonishing statement:

Then the word of God spread, and the number of the disciples *multiplied greatly* in Jerusalem. (Acts 6:7 NKJV)

What was so astonishing? Say these words aloud: "multiplied greatly." Think of this! These words were not used after Peter's classic message resulting in three thousand being born again on the day of Pentecost. No, the word *added* is used (see Acts 2:41). In describing daily conversions, we again see the word *added* (see Acts 2:47). It's the same for the five thousand giving their lives to Jesus a short while later (see Acts 4:4).

The word *multiplied* is not used until the sixth chapter of Acts, when all the church became active in building the kingdom.

Today, multiplication happens when people like Stan, Mike, Phil, Riley, and Dave get into their place of serving and use their gifts. This is when we hear about *great multiplication*.

THE CRITICAL ELEMENT

Now do you understand the critical ingredient for effective multiplication? Think again about our friends Riley and Dave in the light of what we've seen from Scripture. This one couple, who has implemented inspired strategies and served well, have already impacted tens of thousands of people. They have become great according to the words of Jesus. The same is true for Stan, Mike, Phil, and Dana. They all carry the trait of being true servants.

However, please hear these important words: *You can multiply selfishly,* but your impact will not be eternal. There are people who are multiplying, but will one day see all their efforts burned up, because they are motivated by personal gain. This is illustrated in the parable Jesus told of the man who built bigger silos. The man smugly congratulated himself by saying, "Be at ease, eat, drink, and be merry, for I have arrived and now possess all I need and more." But this story did not end well, as all his accomplishments vanished in a moment.

The core message of this book isn't intended to give you the faith to multiply for the purpose of heaping treasures on yourself, but rather to encourage you to give your life in service to others. Jesus declares that when we do this, all the *things* unbelievers pursue will simply be added to us (see Matthew 6:33). I know this, for I've experienced it firsthand.

Let's return to Lisa's and my story regarding our first church. As a result of being in this toxic environment for six years, I had lingering unhealthy attitudes about multiplication. Soon after I left, one of the many transforming and freeing encounters with the Holy Spirit occurred one morning as I was driving my car. He said, "Son, don't seek Me for the blessings. Let Me give them to you."

I immediately thought of Matthew 6:33: "Seek the Kingdom of God above all else, and live righteously, and He will give you everything you need." The Spirit's words brought proper perspective and helped eradicate residual selfish tendencies.

Oh, I'm so grateful to Him. I know what it is like to be selfish and covetous—the unhappiness, the stress, and the distance from the presence of God. Having learned His way and His heart—to seek first building the kingdom—has brought so much joy, peace, and His presence into everyday life!

X

We now have come to the point where we should ask: How do we multiply when we are not the leader of our own work, but serve on someone else's team? Let's answer that in the next chapter, and in doing so, we will see the great benefits.

REFLECT

1. Jesus identifies serving as the path to true greatness. How did Jesus demonstrate serving? What were the results of His serving? How does God's path to greatness differ from the world's?

2. Recall Rebekah's story. What were the remarkable traits involved with her serving?

3. You can multiply selfishly, but your impact will not be eternal. What is the difference between serving to *get* and serving to *give*? Why is it important to serve unselfishly?

I urge you, imitate me. For this reason . . .

—1 Corinthians 4:16–17 NKJV

11

Imitate Me

Before we move on to discuss what hinders multiplication and what fosters it, we have one more important area to discuss. How do we multiply when we are employed by or serving someone else? Which for many of us—much of the time—is exactly where we find ourselves.

To discuss this, I'll focus on the specific area of ministry, but these principles apply to any position you may hold in the corporate world, marketplace, education, healthcare, government, media, athletics, the arts, and any other place in today's world.

Paul states, "It is required in stewards that one be found faithful" (1 Corinthians 4:2 NKJV). As we've established from Scripture, one of the chief characteristics of being faithful is to multiply. A few verses later in his letter, Paul sets up a key component to mass multiplication. He writes:

> For though you might have ten thousand instructors in Christ, yet you do not have *many* fathers; for in Christ Jesus I have begotten you through the gospel. (1 Corinthians 4:15 NKJV)

Paul is a *father* to the Corinthian church. As stated in this verse, a *father* is certainly one who leads another to faith. However, a father can be defined in other ways. In Scripture, a father is more frequently defined as one who is not involved in conversion.

This same Paul, in speaking to the Galatian church, makes this statement: "I advanced in Judaism beyond many of my contemporaries in my own nation, being more exceedingly zealous for the traditions of my *fathers*" (Galatians 1:14 NKJV). Paul isn't referring to any one person as he uses the word *fathers*. This also confirms his statement "you do not have *many* fathers." The word *many* is defined in the Greek as "much of number." This shows we can have more than one "father" in our life.

Paul frequently refers to Timothy as his "son." However, he did not lead Timothy to salvation, for we read that Paul went "to Lystra, where there was a young *disciple* named Timothy. His mother was a Jewish believer, but his father was a Greek. Timothy was well thought of by the believers in Lystra and Iconium" (Acts 16:1–2). It's clear, Timothy was already an established believer when Paul first met him.

If we look at the Old Testament, David refers to his very harsh and tough leader as "my father" (see 1 Samuel 24:11), and Elisha refers to his leader as "my father" (2 Kings 2:12). Elijah says he's not any better than his "fathers" (see 1 Kings 19:4 NKJV), and the long list continues.

For the theme of this book, it is not my intention to elaborate on *what a father is,* but rather to show *who a father can represent.* A father is one who brings leadership, nurturing, and culture to an individual or organization. For the purposes of our discussion, a father could hold a variety of positions: the business owner you work for, your department leader, your pastor, your small group leader, the overseer of your movement, your teacher, your coach, the doctor you serve—and that's the short list. Of course, you probably have concluded that a "father" in these situations could easily be female. Therefore, in referencing fathers I'm also including women who stand in this role.

DIFFERENT OPERATIONS

Paul, as the father of the Corinthian church, instructs in the next verse: "Therefore I urge you, imitate me" (1 Corinthians 4:16 NKJV).

Paul doesn't say, "Imitate me, just as I also imitate Christ." (He does say this later in the eleventh chapter.) However, here the instruction is to simply "imitate me." There is a good reason for this and it's revealed in the next statement:

> *For this reason* I have sent Timothy to you, who is my beloved and *faithful* son in the Lord, who will remind you of *my ways in Christ*, as I teach everywhere in every church. (1 Corinthians 4:17 NKJV)

His initial words, "For this reason," are significant. Paul has just told his readers to imitate him. And, to ensure that there aren't any disconnects in vision, methods, culture, and convictions, he is sending his *faithful* son. What is the indicator of a *faithful* son? *A faithful son or daughter will multiply the ways of his or her father!* I'll address this in more detail shortly, but first, consider this: Paul doesn't write to the Corinthian church saying that Timothy "will remind you of the apostle Peter's ways in Christ." Was Peter an authentic leader in the church? Most definitely. Was he a godly and anointed leader? Again, yes. He has two books in the Bible! Was Peter an apostle for a longer amount of time than Paul? Again, yes.

Additionally, Paul does not write that Timothy "will remind you of the apostle James's ways in Christ." As with Peter, James was a genuine father in the church, had been an apostle longer than Paul, and was a reliable leader. He also has a book in the Bible and served as a lead overseer of the church in Jerusalem.

Did both Peter and James operate differently than Paul? Yes. So then, did Paul's writings and ways make Peter and James's invalid? Absolutely not! However, their ways were not fitting for the Corinthian church where Paul was the spiritual father.

Paul was in the process of establishing his culture in the Corinthian church. His methods were different from the other "fathers," but they were all true to the fundamental beliefs and teachings of Christ. Still, each of them had different methods, ways, and convictions they held for accomplishing the task of making disciples of all nations.

This highlights a truth that many believers are unfamiliar with—a lack of awareness that is often the source of damaging divisions among the body of Christ. Here's the truth: There are different *operations* in the church. In other words, there are different ways of accomplishing the same goal of advancing the kingdom.

Paul instructs the Corinthian church:

There are distinctive varieties of operation [of working to accomplish things], but it is the same God Who inspires and energizes them all in all. (1 Corinthians 12:6 AMPC)

In traveling in ministry on a full-time basis for thirty years, I have witnessed firsthand the variety of cultures, methods, and convictions in the global church. Yet, I can sense the presence of Jesus in each atmosphere.

Paul frequently uses military terms to instruct the church. It's not just imagery; we truly are members of God's military on the earth. I'll follow his lead in illustrating the different operations of ministries. Our United States military consists of diverse branches. We have the Army, Navy, Air Force, Marine Corps, Coast Guard, and Space Force. These branches have different procedures and methods to accomplish their goals and responsibilities. These branches, however, are on the same side when it comes to protecting and serving our nation.

An Air Force cadet will be specifically trained as a functioning member of the United States Air Force. A good amount of instructional emphasis will relate to air tactical operations, for her branch of service operates mainly in the sky. If this cadet happened to be reassigned to the Navy, she would require new training. Of course, there are numerous fundamental techniques that overlap both branches. However, since the Navy operates primarily at sea, this former member of the Air Force would have to learn many new operational maneuvers and military strategies.

It is similar in the kingdom of God. Here's a hypothetical illustration. Let's say the names of your lead pastors are Joe and Terri Anderson. They and their team of leaders have, by God's grace, grown the church to eighteen hundred members, and in doing so, have established ways—methods and culture—that are unique to their leadership style. Your church's fruitfulness has affected your community in a remarkable way. It has local recognition, but that's as far as it goes.

Now, in another location, let's say there is a very popular church that is home to tens of thousands of members with global recognition. Their lead pastors' names are Kevin and Marissa Smith. They are setting trends and leading with fresh new tactics of ministry that are influencing many more people than your pastors. Whose ways are you going to follow, the Smiths or your pastors, the Andersons?

You may be tempted to follow the ways of the popular global leaders and try to sway your leaders to adopt their methods. If you yield to this temptation, I would say you are not being a faithful servant of Jesus Christ but, instead, are fostering disunity, division, or even dissension. You, like the Corinthians, should seek to know and follow your leaders' methods and culture for the sake of unity. The reality is that the Smiths are not your leaders. The Andersons are.

During my years of global travel, observing the body of Christ from more of a bird's-eye view, I've witnessed frequent tragedies resulting from the unawareness of this foundational truth. I've observed those who have gone to leadership or Bible training schools that have a different culture than the church they grew up in. Often these schools are connected to a large church, which sets the overall culture. The students experience the operations of the church in both the school and in their weekend worship experiences.

After graduation, the students return home full of passion and begin efforts to change their home church's culture and methods. While they may be correct believing that the ways they learned are more relevant and effective, if they are too persistent, they can easily become a hindrance to the overall unity of the home church's mission.

If the suggested methods of the former students are refused by the organization, it would be best for all involved for the students to pray and ask God whether they should move on to another church, or submit wholeheartedly to the culture and methods of their leader.

If they move on, they should do so in a manner that would not hurt their former church. It's usually best, in fact, if they move away from the region. God can always bring another leader to the area who can start fresh, and avoid pulling people away from the original church due to existing relationships.

FAITHFUL SON

Now let's address the fact that the apostle Paul calls Timothy a "faithful son." As already stated, a faithful son will seek to multiply the ways of his father. Most likely you have gifts that your leader doesn't have; the question becomes: Are you multiplying your gifts in line with his heart? Does the underlying motive of your multiplication coincide with his convictions and culture, or are you fighting to establish your own way that is counterproductive and contrary to his heart?

How does this play out practically? In two ways—first, by seeking to use your gifts in order to replicate an outcome of your leader if he were in your position with your unique gifts. This doesn't mean you should compromise your specific assignment by becoming a clone of your leader. Here's what I mean: Let's assume you are the youth pastor. You will not reach the young people of your community by cloning your pastor's Sunday morning service.

It's wise to adapt your service in a way that reaches young people, but at the same time doing so with your father's heart. This can only be accomplished through communication with him. There should be open discussions of your strategies and methods. When listening to his responses, you should hear his responses and see how his heart fits within your parameters.

In order to do this effectively, there needs to be open and honest conversation. If you find yourself implementing something you "hope he doesn't notice or hear about," you already know you're heading down a destructive path. If you have doubts, bring them to him; be specific so he can hear exactly what your concerns are. It may be wise to request that he sit in a service. If he struggles with your methods, tell him the "why" behind them. If he's still uncomfortable, then immediately seek out an agreeable plan.

The second way this plays out is by reproducing yourself. Let's assume you run the biggest youth group in the city. That's great; God is blessing your methods, and His gift on your life is drawing people. But are you finding others with similar gifts and imparting to them the wisdom and ways you've learned? Are you raising up several potential youth pastors? By doing so, if your "father" declares the church will now start a new campus in another section of town, you already have people trained and ready to go. I believe one of the reasons many churches can't start campuses in other parts of the city, or plant new churches in another region, is that those in positions under the lead pastor are not reproducing themselves.

You could be the best sound engineer, video editor, children's pastor, worship leader, guitarist, communicator, usher, or one of many other staff positions, but this alone doesn't define true kingdom success. True significance lies in reproducing yourself. Ask yourself, *Am I praying for and searching out others with similar gifts to mine?* Once you've located them, are you teaching, training, and drawing their gifts out while imparting your father's heart to them?

These are the two ways to be faithful when we serve another's vision. We must remember that Jesus emphatically states, "If you have not been faithful in what is another man's, who will give you what is your own?" (Luke 16:12 NKJV).

Let's repeat Jesus's words by using His own definition of faithful: "If you have not multiplied what is another man's, who will give you your own?" Or, "If you have not multiplied your leader's ways, culture, strength, vision, resources and, most of all, heart, who will give you what is your own?" Let's say it still another way: "If you haven't given your entire strength, intellect, energy, and heart to expand your area of responsibility, who will give you your own ministry?" This is sobering when said in these ways.

In my travels, those whom I meet that are successful were originally faithful with what belonged to someone else. I've frequently asked how they started out. I've never found anyone who's experiencing true success now who wasn't first faithful in what belonged to their father or fathers.

MY GREATEST STRUGGLE

When I was young in ministry, my greatest struggle was a hidden insecurity driving me to want to be known and important. I had to prove to others, and mostly myself, that I was a leader with original ideas. I've since learned many potential leaders wrestle with this insecurity, and if not dealt with at the heart level, it later can lead to their downfall.

I was a youth pastor in a large city for one of the fastest-growing churches in the nation, and our team had thought of a way to reach every high school student in the city. It was a unique and very good plan. Our youth group's future would entirely revolve around this initiative, for which my assistants and I had taken eight months to develop a strategy. I had shared the vision with our youth group and they'd embraced it.

But close to the launch of the plan, I discovered it was contrary to my pastor's heart. He asked that we not execute the program. I argued with him for approximately twenty minutes, but he didn't budge. I couldn't think of anything else to say, so I finally shut my mouth—but I was furious. Eight months of work down the drain, a great plan scrapped, but worst of all, our whole vision was built around this program. We had to completely start over. How would I tell our twenty-four leaders and the entire youth group? They'd worked so hard.

Devastated, I went to Lisa for comfort. After rehearsing my frustrations, she sweetly countered, "Well, John, it looks like God is trying to teach you something." Now I was angry with both my pastor and my wife!

I proceeded to get away from Lisa, as in my eyes, she wasn't being supportive. I thought this was the greatest plan ever to reach so many lost high school students. *My pastor and wife must be totally blind*; at least, that is what I thought! I felt alone and frustrated and was definitely inconsolable. At one point, I even thought it was a nightmare and that soon I would wake up and all would be normal again. *Could this really be happening?*

In that moment, God spoke so clearly to my heart. He said, "Son, when I judge you for your time of being youth pastor, I will not first judge how many young people you won to Me. I will first judge how *faithful* you were to the man I put over you."

Those words riveted me, but not nearly as much as His next statement. He firmly said in my heart, "You can win every high school student in the entire city to Me and lose all credit and rewards for your labor because you were *unfaithful* to your pastor."

I suddenly began to tremble in holy fear. I immediately repented and asked forgiveness and called my pastor and did the same with him. After I hung up and pondered what had just transpired, the Lord suddenly gave me a vision. I saw myself moping into the meeting with our twenty-four leaders. I was heavy and sad, and with disgust in my voice announced, "Guys, you know we've worked on this for months; it's the vision of our youth group, but our senior pastor just nixed the program. Everything we've been working toward is no more."

I saw their heads drop in disgust, others' eyes and mouths wide open in disbelief. They were all shocked and upset. I knew in this vision that they were all angry with our lead pastor and saw all of us as victims of his lack of creativity.

God asked me if that was what I intended to do. I responded, "No, Sir! No, Sir! No, Sir!" I knew He was addressing my attitude and heart posture. This vision that He'd given me showed that I still didn't have my father's heart. I immediately repented on a deeper level.

I remember a few days later walking into the meeting with my leaders. Now that I had a holy fear burning in my heart, I had a skip in my step, a twinkle in my eye, and a spark in my voice. I said with great enthusiasm, "Guys, I've got great news! Our lead pastor has spared us from birthing an Ishmael. He has declared that what we've been working on is not the direction he wants this church to go, so we are scrapping the program!"

They all immediately responded with joy. Some smiled, others high-fived each other, and the rest gave a shout of approval. They each caught my heart, because I had finally caught my pastor's heart.

A year later, I was tested again with another significant project we'd worked on for a few months. This time my pastor was aware of it and had agreed with our direction. However, he changed his mind three months into the project. Again, it was a drastic course change, and he was apologetic. I handled it with a totally different attitude than before. I canceled it, didn't push back, argue, or voice disagreement. I distinctly remember the difference I felt; the satisfaction of being able to agree, when in fact, I would have stuck to the original plan if it had been my choice.

Once again, I presented to my leaders the cancellation of our project, as though it had been my own idea. God blessed our youth group. It multiplied three times in size during the two years I held the position.

I'm convinced I would not be where I am today if I had failed these tests. I can tell you what would have transpired, because the Holy Spirit has shown me. I eventually would have canceled the program because I wouldn't have had any choice. I would have done so with an attitude that would have spread to my leaders, thus poisoning them. Eventually I would have left the church and, because of the gifts on my life, would have impacted a small number of people. But I never would have had the ministry we now have, speaking and writing to millions of people globally. Why? Because I was not faithful in what was another's, and I would not have been entrusted with a God-given mission.

It wasn't easy to learn this. As I was a leader with a type A personality, my tendency would have been to fight for what I thought was best. But I learned that God was more concerned about my character than my results. He wanted a firm foundation set in place before He entrusted Lisa and me with our own mission.

My dear friend, you too are a leader. If we walk in His way, God has promised all of His children leadership opportunities. We are "the head and not the tail," we are "above only and not beneath" (see Deuteronomy 28:13 NKJV). Please don't kick against the goads, as I did. Learn from me so you, too, can advance in kingdom responsibility.

THE IMPORTANCE OF UNITY

An organization must be united in order to multiply. One of the most eye-opening portions of Scripture is found in the book of Genesis. A group of ungodly people purposed to do something that was almost unattainable for the people of their time—to build a tower into the heavens. Yet, listen to what God Almighty says:

> Indeed the people are *one* and they all have *one* language, and this is what they begin to do; now *nothing that they propose to do will be withheld* from them. (Genesis 11:6 NKJV)

Remember who is doing the speaking here: it's God Himself. Listen to His words, "Nothing that they propose to do will be withheld." Why did God make such a statement? Because they were "one" and had "one" language. They were unified. They walked together in agreement.

If this is spoken out of the mouth of God in regard to unsaved people, what does He say to covenant people? It's even better, for when His people unite together, it is, "there the LORD commanded the blessing" (Psalm 133:3 NKJV). The word *commanded* means "to order, to direct, to appoint."[13] There's no wiggle room; unity draws blessing, which includes multiplication.

This applies so much more for His New Testament children! No wonder we repeatedly see statements like:

Make me truly happy by *agreeing wholeheartedly* with each other, loving one another, and working together with *one mind* and *purpose*. (Philippians 2:2)

Become complete. Be of good comfort, be of *one mind*, live in peace; and the God of love and peace will be with you. (2 Corinthians 13:11 NKJV)

Only let your conduct be worthy of the gospel of Christ, so that whether I come and see you or am absent, I may hear of your affairs, that you stand fast in *one spirit*, with *one mind* striving together for the faith of the gospel. (Philippians 1:27 NKJV)

We are hearing pleas from the *father* of these churches. Paul is using phrases like "agreeing wholeheartedly," "one mind," "one spirit." He wants to position these churches to be on the receiving end of God's commanded blessing. He knows that only then will they truly multiply in all aspects.

Here is an excellent example of the commanded blessing reserved for those who unify: Jesus's faithful followers obeyed His command to remain in the upper room (see Acts 1:4). During the forty days after His resurrection, Jesus appeared to at least 500 men and women (see 1 Corinthians 15:6); yet ten days after his ascension, only 120 remained in Jerusalem. Where were the others? I conclude that over 75 percent of them didn't listen to Jesus's words. We may not know where they were, but we do know His desire was not their priority.

The men and women in the upper room were unified under the authority of God's Word. The question then became, How would they respond to Peter, His delegated authority, the church *father* Jesus had put in charge?

In the gospels, Peter was often impulsive and out of sync with God's will. When he boldly stated that Jesus was the Christ, the Son of the living God, Jesus declared Peter to be blessed. But within moments, Jesus "turned and said to Peter, 'Get behind Me, Satan! You are an offense to Me, for you are not mindful of the things of God, but the things of men'" (Matthew 16:23 NKJV).

On another occasion, Peter walked on water while the other disciples just observed. He was leading the way once again. But within moments, he began sinking. Jesus lamented by saying, "O you of little faith, why did you doubt?" (Matthew 14:31 NKJV).

In still another incident, Peter, along with John and James, was escorted by Jesus to the mountain of transfiguration. There they witnessed His face shining like the sun and even His clothing being transformed. Moses and Elijah appeared and talked with Jesus. What an honor! Yet, before Jesus and the three disciples descended the mountain, Peter blurted out that they should build tabernacles—two of them for Elijah and Moses (see Matthew 17). Again, he was out of sync with God's plans and purposes.

With this in mind, let's examine one of Peter's first decisions as a leader of the inaugural church. Before we do, however, we must remember one other important fact: At this moment, only days have passed since Peter had denied that he even knew Jesus. This normally would give many men and women permission to not heed Peter's leadership, especially if they disagreed with his direction or decisions.

So let's set the stage. A few days had passed since Jesus's ascension, and Peter found a prophetic word in the book of Psalms that directly related to the events of Judas's betrayal of Jesus. Peter read to the small congregation in the upper room: "This was written in the book of Psalms, where it says, . . . 'Let *someone else take his position*.'" (Acts 1:20). Once again Peter saw what others didn't, but would he handle it correctly?

What you're about to read can certainly be viewed as speculative, but I hope to give enough scriptural support to make my point valid. I believe that, once again, Peter was out of sync with God in his decision-making, for he suggested that they round up all the men who'd been with them from the beginning so they could "cast lots" in order to see who God would choose to take Judas's position.

Nowhere in the New Testament will you find God picking an apostle by a lottery system! Jesus showed these men God's way by leaving them an example: He prayed all night and heard from God before he chose the twelve original apostles (see Luke 6:12–13). It would have been best if Peter had sought to acquire the next apostle in a manner more similar to Jesus.

Remember, just a few years later, the prophets and teachers in the church in Antioch followed Jesus's example. They fasted and prayed before Barnabas and Saul were separated to the office of apostle (see Acts 13:1–4). This is yet another confirmation of the error of Peter's hasty decision.

The 120 in the upper room found two candidates: Matthias and Justus. Matthias won the lottery and was numbered among the apostles (see Acts 1:23–26); however, you never find Matthias's name again in the New Testament. Why? Because Scripture would show that Paul was God's choice to replace Judas, not Matthias. This is why Paul wrote:

He [Jesus] was seen by James and later by all the apostles. Last of all, as though I had been born at the wrong time, I also saw Him. For I am the least of all the apostles. (1 Corinthians 15:7–9)

Paul referred to himself as though he had been born at the wrong time; in other words, he was probably too young to be one of the original twelve. In my research, I've found different opinions of the dates of Paul's birth; the estimates from different sources range as high as fourteen years. One thing is certain; no one knows his birth year. So let's look at the time line of the New Testament to get a glimpse of his age.

By most accounts, Stephen's martyrdom occurred four years after Jesus's resurrection, which means Jesus had chosen His original group of disciples seven years earlier. During Stephen's stoning, Scripture refers to Saul (Paul) as a "young man" (see Acts 7:58). The *Greek–English Lexicon* states the Greek word for "young man" refers to someone just after puberty. So in subtracting the seven years, it's fairly safe to assume Paul was too young to be an original disciple.

I fully believe Paul was God's choice. He clearly possessed the fruit and authority of an apostle, much more so than Matthias. The main point: I believe Peter made an impulsive leadership decision that was out of sync with God's plan. If he made this move in today's modern church, we most likely would have had a three-way church split: the "anti-lottery apostle picking" group, the "there's no need for new apostles" group, and the "lottery-picking apostle" group (which would have remained). Yet, listen to the very next words recorded in Scripture after this incident:

When the Day of Pentecost had fully come, they were all with *one accord* in one place. (Acts 2:1 NKJV)

The words *one accord* are actually one Greek word, *homothumadon*. It is defined as, "with one mind, with unanimous consent, in one accord, all together."[14] From this definition, there is no room for division, either mentally or behaviorally. They were united in purpose, mind, heart, and spirit. What was the result? Scripture states that three thousand were *added* to the Lord that day! If you divide this number by 120, you end up with *multiplication* of twenty-five times.

Think of it—the church grew twenty-five times in just one service. God commanded His blessing on their unity! It is a spiritual law.

I'm sure there were some believers in the upper room who would have done things differently than Peter. No doubt a better choice would have been to follow Jesus's example and first seek God for an extended time before making the decision.

Even though there was a better way of going about it, the people in that room saw the higher priority—to remain *one* by owning their leader's strategy. Each proceeded forward as if it had been his or her idea. How often do we divide over the silliest or smallest disagreements in our methods? (Let me interject this one important truth: If your leader makes a decision that is categorized by Scripture as a *sin*, this is the only time we are told not to adhere. However, most fallouts occur over methods, not sin.)

UNDERTOWS

We must remember that dissension is not limited to words or actions; it goes deeper—to the mind, heart, and spirit. Look at the three prior Scriptures once again as a refresher. We can be united outwardly but divided in our motives and thoughts.

My mother lives in Vero Beach, Florida. Approximately thirteen miles north of her residence is a place called Sebastian's Inlet. It is known to the locals for its strong undertows. An undertow is a phenomenon that is not noticeable to the naked eye. All the water on top of the ocean surface appears to be flowing in one direction, moving in unison toward the beach. Yet underneath the surface, water is moving swiftly in the opposite direction. This contrary current grabs its victims and pulls them out to sea, sometimes taking their lives.

Are there undertows in our churches, businesses, schools, governments, athletic teams, and clubs that bring the destructive prevention of multiplication? Absolutely yes. Why is this? Is it because we are attempting to build the kingdom of God with a democratic mindset rather than a kingdom mindset? We are citizens of a real kingdom, and our King's delegated authority cannot be overlooked. His blessing manifests when we are submitted in heart to our leaders.

We must ask ourselves, *Is it more important that we are right or that we are one*? You can be 100 percent right, but 100 percent wrong at the same time. If there had been a coalition petitioning to override Peter's choice of a lottery system to replace it with fasting and prayer (according to the pattern we've seen in Scripture), the coalition would have been 100 percent correct. However, because of their disunity, the outpouring of God's blessing was stopped.

If you recall, the first-time *extraordinary multiplication* occurred in Scripture was after the fathers had given an operational directive. Afterward we read, "Everyone in the church loved this idea" (Acts 6:5 TPT). What was the result? "The number of the disciples *multiplied greatly*" (Acts 6:7 NKJV). Everyone in the organization owned it as if it was their strategy. Again, I'm sure people could have objected, but they had discovered a truth: *It was better to be blessed than it was to be right*. So, they embraced the method as if it was their own idea.

Now we must ask the most difficult question: How many of us will stand before Jesus at the judgment seat, shocked and bewildered by what He reveals? Will He show us, with tears, how our undertow contribution hindered the commanded blessing? Will we see the lives that would have been impacted for eternity and weep with Him as we realize the missed opportunity for us to multiply? How many of us will wish to go back and seek to be unified, as opposed to being right? But it will be too late.

REFLECT

1. A father is one who brings leadership, nurture, and culture to an individual or organization—and they can hold a variety of positions: CEO, pastor, small group leader, department leader, boss, teacher, coach (these are just a few examples). Who are father figures in your life? In what ways have they been a father to you?

2. A faithful son or daughter will multiply the ways of his or her father. Why is it important to imitate the ways of your leaders? How does this ensure that there aren't disconnects in vision, methods, and culture?

3. Multiplying what belongs to another requires that you reproduce yourself. Are you finding others with similar gifts and imparting to them the wisdom and ways you've learned? Are you raising up others to do what you are doing at present? If not, how can you begin to do so?

Master, I knew you were a harsh man, *harvesting crops you didn't plant and gathering crops you didn't cultivate. I was* afraid *I would lose your money, so I hid it in the earth.*

—Matthew 25:24–25

12

Hindrances to Multiplication I

Now we'll dive into the motives and thoughts of the lazy steward of Jesus's parable. Why did the other two servants multiply and he only maintained? Why were servants one and two identified as "good and faithful," while he was referred to as "wicked and lazy"?

Before continuing, let's take some time to first establish a truth: *When someone stands in the presence of Jesus, it's impossible to lie.* Why am I mentioning this here? Let me explain with a trivial illustration. Have you ever watched an espionage movie and at one point during an interrogation, a "truth serum" is administered to expose hidden realities? The spy or double agent then reveals what he was sworn to conceal; the truth is uncovered.

Let's turn to a real-life situation. In our early years of marriage, I was immature and insecure. There were incidents in which I behaved in a way that seemed acceptable at the time, until Lisa confronted me. In our discussions, I strongly defended my actions and motives. Often in those discussions, I'd boldly defend the accuracy of my statements! Later, while in prayer and in the presence of God, I'd realize she was spot on. I would return to Lisa in humility and admit my error.

The point: Deception, dishonesty, trickery, duplicity, and other similar behaviors cannot coexist in the royal presence of God. Jesus states:

The time is coming when everything that is covered up will be
revealed, and all that is secret will be made known to all. Whatever you have said in the dark will be heard in the light, and
what you have whispered behind closed doors will be shouted
from the housetops for all to hear! (Luke 12:2–3)

Jesus is speaking specifically of the judgment when it will be impossible to think or speak in a deceiving manner, for truth will per-
meate the atmosphere and no lie or deceitful word will be uttered. The
very fact that our stewardship parable represents the judgment means
that we can be confident that the answer given by the lazy servant is
accurate. He exposes himself, even when it accuses him.

There are two major factors behind why he didn't *eternally*
multiply:

- He did not know the character of His master.
- He was afraid.

These two reasons are given in order. The second is often, but not
always, precipitated by the first, as ignorance of the character of God
easily fosters fear. This will be made clear as we continue to unpack
both errors.

"WHAT I BELIEVE"

As we unpack the first error, let me tell a story. I had just flown eight
hours to Hawaii for a conference. Still in my travel clothes, waiting for
my hotel room to be ready, I'd found a spot to rest under a poolside
umbrella. It just so happened that a businesswoman was also waiting—she was attending a different conference. We got to talking, and
once she discovered I was a Christian author and minister, she began
to elaborate on her relationship with God.

It didn't take more than a minute or two to realize that she didn't know God. She kept confidently stating what she *believed* and very little corresponded to what Scripture reveals. While she was still expounding further on her beliefs, I asked the Holy Spirit for wisdom, and He showed me what to say.

When the woman finished her discourse, I asked, "Do you see the man sitting across the pool?"

"Why, yes," she responded.

"Allow me to tell you about him," I said. "He's a strict vegan—he doesn't eat anything from an animal, not even honey. His dream is to be on the United States Olympic Swim Team. He works out and practices three hours a day. His hobbies are racquetball, tennis, skydiving, and painting. He's married to that woman just over there by the hot tub, and she's ten years younger than he."

The woman was intrigued but also a little confused as to why I would change the subject so abruptly. She had just shared her deep thoughts of God and, in turn, suddenly I am describing a man across the pool. Her curiosity got the best of her, so she asked, "Is he here to attend the conference with you?"

"No, ma'am."

"Well, how do you know him?" she asked, even more curious.

"I've never met him."

Now looking confused and concerned, she asked how I knew so much about him. I have no idea if this is correct, but by the look on her face, I'm guessing she might have thought I was a CIA operative, an FBI agent, a detective, or even a stalker. Her curiosity had been piqued.

I paused, and then said to her, "That's what I *believe* about him."

She was speechless.

"You just spoke with such confidence of your *belief* of who God is," I continued. "But almost everything you just said about Him is not true. I know this because I know Him."

Then I turned, looked her straight in the eye, and said, "What I just did with that man who I've never met before is no different than what you just did with God. I told you what I *believe* about the man across the pool, and I sounded quite convincing. But chances are that most of what I said isn't true, and the reason is, I've never taken the time to get to know him."

The woman was listening but appeared slightly shaken.

"God gave us His Word, recorded on the pages of the Bible, that reveal who He is," I said calmly. "He also sent His Spirit to reveal Jesus to us, who in turn shows us God Almighty, because He is God manifested in the flesh."

I paused, and then asked gently, "Do you think you may have made up an imaginary God in your mind, one who actually doesn't exist?"

Sadly, either she was not ready to confront her lack of knowing God or she was scared to face the reality of meeting Him. We chatted for a few more minutes and soon afterward parted ways.

You may be smiling as you read this story, as you think, *I know God. I go to church and I have read the Bible.* However, before any of us get too comfortable in that thought, we must remember the plight of the Pharisees. They had perfect church attendance, prayed and fasted regularly, and could quote from memory the first five books of the Bible. (I sure don't have that good a record!) Yet, they couldn't recognize God manifested in the flesh—Jesus, standing right before them.

KNOWING GOD

Who gets the privilege of knowing God? All are invited, but there are established parameters. The door is open for an authentic relationship when we, from the core of our being, make the decision to give our life fully to Him. Not in pretense, but accompanied with corresponding actions. Jesus says, "If you give up your life for my sake, you will save it" (Matthew 16:25). What does He mean by "save it"? It's simple; true life is only found in *knowing Him*.

We don't come to know God by attending church, surrounding ourselves with Christian friends, reading books, listening to worship music, repeating a "salvation" prayer, or even by doing good works. In Scripture Jesus is frequently referred to as the Groom, and we are referred to as the bride. When a bride and groom unite, the two become one. Paul writes, "*It is an illustration* of the way Christ and the church are one" (Ephesians 5:32). To show what knowing Him is like, God gave us an *illustrated sermon*, one that is most common among mankind. On a daily basis, a clear representation of a relationship with Him can be observed: *marriage. Holy matrimony.*

When a woman walks down an aisle of a church in a white dress to the wedding march, she is making a very strong statement. She is saying good-bye to roughly the other 3,930,000,000 men in the world! She is giving her entire heart, soul, body, and life to the one man waiting for her at the altar. Interestingly, her decision represents true "repentance." She is walking away from all opportunities to establish a marriage union with all the rest of the men on earth. She and her chosen husband enter a covenant: He is entirely hers; she is entirely his. The two embark on a journey that carries the potential of a deepening relationship, of knowing each other more than they could ever know anyone else.

Now I want to say something that may appear controversial, but hear me out! I personally believe one of the great obstacles we've created to *knowing* God is the introduction of the "sinner's prayer." Our tradition typically looks like this: We sell a relationship with God almost as if we are marketing a product to a consumer. After a message or conversation, we say, "Do you want to know God? Do you want a relationship with your Creator? Then just pray this prayer: 'Jesus, come into my life. I receive You as my Savior. Thank You for forgiving me and now making me a child of God.'"

Next, we announce the happy news to all who are present, celebrate that our new converts are forever secure with God, and invite them into our fellowship. However, we've said nothing about repentance—their need to walk away permanently from a self-seeking lifestyle and lay down their life for Him. Yet, listen to Jesus's full statement:

> If you truly want to follow Me, you should at once completely reject and disown your own life. And you must be willing to share My cross and experience it as your own, as you continually surrender to My ways. For if you choose self-sacrifice and lose your lives for My glory, you will continually discover true life. But if you choose to keep your lives for yourselves, you will forfeit what you try to keep. (Matthew 16:24–25 TPT)

We can only truly know God by entering an authentic relationship with Him, which is what Jesus summarized in these verses. Knowing God is not a one-time event, but a firm decision to submit to His ways over what you think is best for you. This is a decision that is made day by day, moment by moment. If an issue is clearly revealed in His Word, there is no debating or wiggling out of obedience. Following Jesus means that you've made the decision deep in your heart to walk away from that which offends Him and to serve Him on an ongoing basis.

The apostle James writes, "But don't just listen to God's Word. You must do what it says. Otherwise, you are only fooling yourselves" (James 1:22). The person who hears God's Word, yet is unresponsive in thought, word, and action, has fooled himself. The Passion Translation calls this "self-deception," which I think accurately describes the third steward, the Pharisees, the woman at the pool in Hawaii, and many others I've encountered, who fully believe they are in relationship with God because they attend church and quote Scripture but are regularly speaking and living contrary to His Word. They are sadly misled. It is *self-deception*.

Let me quickly make one important point. Lisa will tell you that she's made many mistakes in our marriage (I've made more, but here I'm focusing on the bride!), but she has never purposefully sought her own desires at the expense of our marriage covenant. Her behavior hasn't been perfect, but her heart has never departed from steadfast loyalty.

Likewise, in our relationship with God, if we periodically disobey, He forgives. This is no different than a husband and wife not breaking their covenant relationship when a mistake is made. A relationship with our Creator is true loyalty from the heart, not lip service without authentic, corresponding actions.

Jesus makes the most remarkable statement: "If anyone *wills* to do His will, he shall *know* . . ." (John 7:17 NKJV). It begins in the core of our being; when we deeply desire to act on, not just hear. We do *whatever* He says and then we *know*. We recognize and *know* God and His word. The Passion Translation renders John 7:17 beautifully: "First be passionate to do God's will, and then you will be able to discern if my teachings are from the heart of God."

In the parable of the talents, all three stewards heard the exact same instructions before the departure of their lord. Two put into action his instructions and one did nothing. It's no coincidence that the third steward really didn't *know* his master, so he regarded the importance of his instructions lightly. This steward was self-deceived.

HOLY FEAR

A biblical phrase describes our discussion thus far: *the fear of the Lord*. Due to all the fear that abounds, especially in this day and hour, we shy away from this statement. However, there are *two fears* and they are totally opposite of each other. One is the "spirit of fear," and the other is the "fear of the Lord." Scripture distinguishes between the two. Moses said to God's people just after they drew back from God's presence:

> "*Do not fear*; for God has come to test you, and that *His fear* may be before you, so that you may not sin." So the people *stood afar off*, but Moses *drew near* the thick darkness where God was. (Exodus 20:20–21 NKJV)

At first glance, it seems Moses contradicts himself. Let me paraphrase his statement to make it clear: "Do not *fear* because God has come to see if His *fear* is in you." His declaration is not a contradiction, rather a differentiating between being "scared of God" and the "fear of the Lord"—there is a difference. The person who is scared of God has something to hide. Recall how Adam hid from the presence of the Lord after he sinned against Him (see Genesis 3:8). On the other hand, the person who fears God has nothing to hide. He or she is actually scared to be away from Him.

So up front, permit me to make a firm point: *The fear of the Lord is not to be scared of God.* How can we have an intimate relationship with Someone we are afraid of? As already stated, true holy fear is to be terrified to be away from God. You don't want to be anywhere other than in His presence, care, and love. You're immovable, no matter the circumstances or how bleak things appear; you know there's no place better than being close to Him. This is evident by your obedience to Him.

To fear God is to venerate, revere, honor, and respect Him more than anyone or anything else. It is to hold Him in the highest esteem, to embrace His heart's desires as more precious and valuable than our own. We love what He loves and we hate what He hates. What is important to Him becomes important to us; what is not so important to Him is not so important to us.

This posture places us among those that are welcomed to be close to Him. If you examine the children of Israel, their love for God was conditional. When circumstances were favorable, they worshipped, obeyed, and loved Him. When unfavorable, they complained. They didn't trust Him implicitly but instead were committed to self-preservation. By seeking to save their own lives, they did the opposite of what Jesus states in the gospel; they forsook the glorious privilege of a genuine relationship with Him. Moses feared God; they didn't.

Their motives manifested accordingly—the people *stood afar off*, but Moses *drew near* to God's presence. They lived a life blind to what was best. In contrast, Moses saw clearly. Moses knew God—His Word, ways, and wisdom. They, on the other hand, only knew God by how He answered their prayers.

We operate appropriately in the fear of the Lord when we obey Him instantly; even if it doesn't make sense, there's no apparent benefit, and perhaps even appears harmful to our well-being. We know His character, and thus are convinced. Even though something may appear detrimental, it will never be so when obeying God.

Lastly, walking in the fear of the Lord manifests by obeying Him to completion. Abraham did exactly this when God told him to let go of what was most important to him—what he'd waited twenty-five years for—to surrender the one he loved more than any person or any possession—his son Isaac. He left early in the morning and made a three-day journey in order to do what God asked of him. God hadn't given him a "why," and it appeared that this sacrifice would ruin all Abraham had lived for. It appeared detrimental. But he implicitly trusted the *character* of God (the very antithesis of how the lazy steward acted).

Once Abraham had the knife raised to execute Isaac, the angel of the Lord stopped him and declared, "Do not hurt him in any way, for now I know that *you truly fear God*. You have not withheld from me even your son, your only son" (Genesis 22:12). This kind of love, trust, and faith is the heart of one who truly fears God.

We are told, "The fear of the LORD is the beginning of knowledge" (Proverbs 1:7 NKJV). What knowledge? We find the answer shortly afterward, but let's also examine what leads up to the answer—putting His Word above all, which is no different than what Abraham did:

> My son, if you receive My words, and treasure My commands within you, so that you incline your ear to wisdom, and apply your heart to understanding; yes, if you cry out for discernment, and lift up your voice for understanding, if you seek her as silver, and search for her as *for* hidden treasures; then you will understand the fear of the LORD, and *find the knowledge of God.* (Proverbs 2:1–5 NKJV)

The answer is quite clear; the fear of the Lord is *the beginning of the knowledge of God.* Today we would phrase it a little differently. We might say, "You will understand the fear of the Lord, and begin to know God intimately." Now we understand the root error of the lazy steward. He lacked holy fear, which was evident by his lack of action and his final response. Just as Israel at times saw God as a tyrant, this steward saw his master no differently. He was blind to his leader's character.

Holy fear is the starting place of *knowing* God. The psalmist confirms this by declaring: "The LORD is a friend to those who fear Him" (Psalm 25:14). Friends are those we know on an *intimate* level. Jesus makes a startling statement, "You show that you are My *intimate* friends when you obey all that I command you" (John 15:14 TPT).

Many of us often say we "love" Jesus in the same way we say we love a famous movie star, athlete, or any publicly known figure. In early 2020, when Kobe Bryant and his daughter Gianna were killed in a tragic helicopter accident, the entire nation mourned and many wept. People placed an abundance of balloons, cards, and flowers near the Staples Center in Los Angeles where he'd played basketball. I also mourned the tragedy and thought quite a bit about it.

But most of us who mourned didn't know Kobe like his wife, family, and close friends did. If he'd seen us on the street, he would have had no idea who we were. I'd never spent time with him, yet I grieved his passing as if I did have a relationship with him. Just as Kobe would not have known me when he was alive, there will be a multitude of men and women claiming to know Jesus because they attended church, spoke of Him on social media, listened to music about Him, did things in His name, and even professed His Lordship. But Jesus's reply will be, "I never knew you." And this is why:

> Not everyone who calls out to Me, "Lord! Lord!" will enter the
> Kingdom of Heaven. Only those who actually do the will of My
> Father in heaven will enter. On judgment day many will say
> to Me, "Lord! Lord! We prophesied in Your name and cast out
> demons in Your name and performed many miracles in Your
> name." But I will reply, "I never knew you. Get away from Me,
> you who break God's laws." (Matthew 7:21–23)

We don't ever want this said to us by the Master. If you examine this Scripture passage closely, these people were confident in their relationship with Jesus, even emotional about it. Kobe would have said to me, "Who are you? Where are you from? What's your name?" In this way, Jesus will say to many claiming to know Him, "I don't know you or where you come from" (Luke 13:25).

SPEND TIME WITH HIM

The fear of the Lord is the starting place of knowing Him intimately, but why camp at the starting place? Go deeper in your relationship, because He's calling you to come closer. We are told, "Come close to God, and God will come close to you" (James 4:8). Amazingly, we determine the level of our relationship with Him.

It surprises me how so many people who are professing believers are not much different than the woman I met at the pool in Hawaii. They get their "knowledge of God" from social media, worship music, blogs, conversations with friends, and their pastor speaking about Him once a week. But they don't spend personal time with Him.

The latest statistics show that people between the ages of fifteen and twenty-five spend 53.7 hours a week in front of screens—smartphones, tablets, computers, and television.[15] I wonder, how much time is spent in the Word of God? And that question is not just relevant to young people!

I've been reading my Bible for over forty years, and it is still one of my favorite things to do. Before reading, I always ask the Holy Spirit to reveal Jesus to me in a fresh way. I've spent years getting up early and spending time pacing around my basement, or outside in a remote place, or in my hotel room—just reading, praying, and listening. I don't want to be one of those who preached the gospel all over the world by relying solely on my gift and never getting to know the Gift-giver.

God wants to be intimate with you. His perfect love casts out fear. Too often we find ourselves acting like the steward who was blind to his master's goodness. This is why I encourage you to pray for God to fill you with His holy fear. Then spend quality time with Him and discover Who He truly is: Love.

God sought us out, loved, and died for us long before we knew Him. He initiated this magnificent relationship. He is for you. He longs to know you intimately. However, He loves us so deeply that He refuses to force us into a relationship.

So choose now! Choose life! Choose to know Him . . . intimately.

REFLECT

1. Fear is always fueled by an ignorance of the character of God. How has an incorrect view of God's nature affected the way you've stewarded your gifts and calling?

2. An authentic relationship with God is made possible when you give yourself fully to Him and live obediently to His Word. Is there any mindset or behavior that is hindering your relationship with God?

3. There's a big difference between *being afraid of God* and *having the fear of the Lord*. What is the difference? Why is having the fear of the Lord critical to knowing God intimately?

Master, I know You have high standards and hate careless ways, that You demand the best and make no allowances for error. I was afraid.

—Matthew 25:24–25 MSG

13

Hindrances to Multiplication II

We are now ready to unpack the lazy steward's second statement, "I was afraid." Fear paralyzed him. I love *The Message's* paraphrase of the third servant's words: "I know You have high standards . . . You demand the best and make no allowances for error."

This reminds me of a story. I played organized basketball under two coaches. On both teams I was a shooting guard, because hitting baskets from fifteen feet to the three-point range was one of the few things in the sport I could do well.

My first coach was a man who wanted the best out of us and would use encouragement and constructive correction to get us there. I knew he was for me, not against me. I made shots from all over the floor with confidence. His belief in me fueled that confidence.

My next coach was different. In his words, he was "one who had high standards and made no allowances for error." When I took a shot and missed, the coach sharply corrected me during the next timeout, and most often I was benched soon afterward. I couldn't shoot well under his coaching. In my personal practice time, when he wasn't present, I nailed shots from all over the floor. I was the same player with the same talent, but I couldn't execute when he was present.

If you look at the servant's response in the above Scripture, his *perception* of the master was exactly the same as I had of my critical coach. But there's a big difference: *In reality*, the servant's master was nothing like my second coach.

Again, following up on what we learned in the last chapter, this is why it's paramount for us to take the time to know God. He is nothing like this lazy steward's *perception*. God is for us; He believes in us and has confidence in us. If we don't *see* Him that way, we can easily succumb to fear and our gifts will be buried.

This all being said, we now turn to an entirely different root cause of unfruitfulness. As mentioned in the previous chapter, there are people who actually do know God but still wrestle with and even succumb to fear. There are reasons for this that Scripture addresses, and we'll expand on this very thing for the rest of this chapter. Before doing so, however, here are some insightful comments on fear and related topics:

> It's not death a man should fear, but he should fear never beginning to live.
> —Marcus Aurelius

> Never be afraid of trying something new. Remember, amateurs built the ark; professionals built the *Titanic*.
> —Unknown

> The greatest mistake we make is living in constant fear we will make one.
> —John C. Maxwell

One of the greatest discoveries a man makes, one of his great surprises, is to find he could do what he was afraid he couldn't do.
—Henry Ford

Let's open our discussion with a statement of unfaltering truth:
The opposite of unhealthy fear is the love of God. When we love God
and people unconditionally, fear is exterminated. As the apostle John
writes, "Perfect love expels all fear" (1 John 4:18).

In regard to this truth, I will never forget an eye-opening encounter I had with the Holy Spirit in San Diego. I'd just finished a service,
was alone in my room, and found myself battling fear in regard to our
sons. I'd heard of ministers' children who had been tragically killed:
one by electrocution, many in car accidents, some by drug overdoses
or drowning, and others for various reasons. I'd just heard of another
tragedy and was trying to eradicate the worry that was hounding me.
Suddenly, I heard in my heart, "Son, fear is an indicator. It merely
exposes an area of your life that you haven't submitted to Me; you still
own that area of your life."

His words riveted me. I realized I had taken on what I didn't have
the power to maintain. Within moments of this enlightenment, I
shouted out in my room, "Father, these sons are not mine. I'm merely
a steward of those who are Yours. Therefore, whatever You desire for
them is what I want to be done in their lives, no matter what. You may
take them halfway around the world and to heaven when You're ready
for them, but I do boldly ask that they fulfill all You created them to
do in this world."

I then shouted even louder, "But, devil, in Jesus's name, you are
not touching them! I declare them to be God's, and I forbid you to kill,
steal, or destroy what is God's!"

An overwhelming peace hit my heart, and I've never worried

about our four sons since. If worry does try to creep back, I sternly say, "I gave the care of our sons to God in San Diego, and I'm not taking it back." Each time, the fear has immediately subsided and the peace has returned.

Fear is a horrible taskmaster. It's sneaky, seeks to gain control, and once it has a grip on you, it's overwhelming. If not properly dealt with, it will alter your destiny. But here's the good news: Fear is beatable but must be addressed properly.

PAY ATTENTION TO YOUR GIFT

Paul wrote two letters to his "spiritual son," Timothy. In both, he addressed the fact that Timothy's gift (*charisma*) was being neglected and was inoperative. Let's establish this important point up front; Timothy was a godly man. Paul bragged on his proven character and genuine faith throughout the epistles. Timothy certainly doesn't fall into the category of one who is paralyzed by fear from not knowing God's character. Paul's first letter states, "Do not *neglect* the gift that is in you" (1 Timothy 4:14 NKJV).

The word *neglect* in the Greek is *ameléō*. A couple of defining words are "to overlook or regard lightly."[16] Another source defines this word as "to not think about, and thus not respond appropriately to—'to pay no attention to.'"[17]

Why would Timothy—or any of us—overlook and not pay attention to a God-given gift, and in an extreme case, not even think about it? One reason could be:

It isn't working or producing
according to our expectations.

The thought becomes, *I tried and it didn't work*. I was often tempted to think this way in my twenties and early thirties. As I wrote about earlier, one occasion came after Lisa and her friend fell asleep during my message. I had this thought: *Why would anyone want to listen to me when those closest to me can't even stay awake?*

Around the same time, another reality that increased my struggle with thoughts of failure, was when a friend and I were each teaching a Sunday school class. He had over two hundred attend his class— standing room only. During this same time frame, my class average attendance was approximately twenty people. There was actually one class I taught during this time period that only one person attended!

There were other occasions, too numerous to list, when I was tempted to question my gifts. I realize now that if I had yielded to these thoughts of unmet expectations and apparent failure, I would have given up on ministry and pursued another path—ultimately becoming miserable because of leaving my life-calling.

Another reason we can overlook and not pay attention to our God-given gift is:

The criticism of others.

Without question, I was sorely tempted to stop writing after my first manuscript was ignored, criticized, and rejected by the first editor and then the publishers. Later, just after I self-published my book, a friend made disparaging remarks about my writing style. After I heard those comments, that evening I lay on our living room floor, not budging for twenty or thirty minutes, staring at the ceiling, feeling overwhelmingly dejected. I wondered if I had wasted an entire year of my life, and a lot of money, on that book! I thought, *The first editor, the publishers, now my friends have all criticized it. Wake up, John! Why can't you just admit it's no good and that you've failed?*

If I had succumbed to these thoughts and other remarks, I would not have written the second book, which also seemed like a failure. I remember sending it to my former Bible school teacher and she sharply criticized it, too—I was even more devastated! It was now two and a half years and neither book had gained any traction.

If at any point I had listened to the criticism of others and my own thoughts of dejection, it would have been so easy to just quit. And I would not have written the third book that was, of course, *The Bait of Satan*.

Another reason we can overlook and not pay attention to our God-given gift is:

The fear of failing.

Here is the ironic reality of this fear: We expect to fail before we ever begin, so we protect ourselves by not even attempting! The thought is, *Why try if it's not going to work?* How many dreams and visions have been thwarted due to the fear of failing? How tragic that God-given gifts are wasted in a manner no different than that of the lazy servant.

Concerning what the fear of failure produces, my friend Myles Munroe wrote in his book *Maximizing Your Potential*:

The graveyard is the richest place on earth, because it is here that you will find all the hopes and dreams that were never fulfilled, the books that were never written, the songs that were never sung, the inventions that were never shared, the cures that were never discovered, all because someone was too afraid to take that first step.[18]

In agreement with Myles, my strong admonition is: Don't allow your God-given gifts to be withheld from expression in this life.

What I will say next may surprise you, since all of us highly regard Timothy. But in Paul's letters we learn that Timothy is heading in the same direction of the lazy steward! His God-given gift was lying dormant and he was not paying attention to it. Fortunately, he had a good father in the faith who wouldn't allow him to continue in this state.

In the second letter that Paul wrote to his "son," he doesn't waste any time and speaks to this issue right out of the gate: "I remind you to *stir up* the gift of God which is in you" (2 Timothy 1:6 NKJV). The words *stir up* in Greek are just one word, *anazōpuréō*, which is defined as "to revive a fire."[19] But the *Greek–English Lexicon* communicates this word's meaning even more fully. It defines this word as "to cause something to begin again—'to reactivate.'"[20] God's gift in Timothy was inactive and needed to be kick-started once again. So how had that dormancy happened? Paul explains the cause in the very next verse:

> For God has not given us a spirit of *fear*, but of power and of love and of a sound mind. (2 Timothy 1:7 NKJV)

The Greek word for *fear* is *deilia*, which is most accurately translated as "timidity." Paul is saying, "Timothy, your God-given gift is dormant due to a spirit of *timidity*," or to put it even more plainly, "Timothy, your God-given gift is inoperative due to a spirit of *intimidation*."

This is a word we can easily relate to. Intimidation means "to be deterred from action due to fear." But the more important aspect is that the ultimate origin of intimidation is *a spirit*. It's a spiritual force, and if we don't address fear on a spiritual level, its roots are not fully cut off.

MY BATTLE WITH INTIMIDATION

I know all about this because I battled this spirit for many years. I assumed it was a weakness in my personality. But during a set of meetings in the early 1990s, I discovered I was completely wrong in my assessment. The meetings were scheduled to last for only four days in a small-town church, but instead they turned into a three-week move of God. Every night, the building was packed to capacity and many were saved, healed, and delivered. The gift of God in my life to preach was in high gear. It was remarkable. People traveled as far as ninety miles to attend the nightly services. I distinctly remember going into the empty sanctuary during the daytime, and it seemed as if God's presence had settled in the building.

But one evening in the final week, this would all change. Some of the worship leaders had criticized my ministry the night before. What they had said was relayed to me by one of the church leaders just before service. The comments seemed opinionated, yet harmless. However, I couldn't shake their words in my thoughts. My focus shifted from the upcoming service to critiquing my message from the previous evening. The pastor dismissed their remarks; we prayed and went into the sanctuary, as we'd done for so many services.

That night everything seemed dry. I tried to minister like I'd done for the previous two weeks, but I was confused, couldn't keep a thought, and hated being on the platform. I wanted to escape out the back door! I felt powerless, like a teenager in a high school speech class miserably failing to communicate before my fellow students. There was no anointing; no presence of God on me. It was horrible. I closed the service early and returned to where I was staying.

I found myself upset with God. *Why didn't He help me? Why was this service so different? Why did I feel abandoned?* I thought, *That message and time of ministry was pathetic. Nobody will come back tomorrow night. In fact, I don't want to go back tomorrow.*

I went to bed with hopes the next day would be different.

The following morning, I woke up heavy, depressed, and discouraged. I tried to pray but to no avail. The concern over what was wrong began to grow. That afternoon, I spent three hours in prayer. I fought thoughts of failure the entire time. I roused myself to push past the heaviness and psyched myself up for the upcoming service.

That night in the sanctuary, the worship felt just as dry as the night before, and I felt I had nothing to give. Again, I wanted to run out the back door. Once introduced, I got up and floundered for a few minutes. I couldn't keep a thought. At one point I heard a voice in my head say, "Why did you say that? Where are you going with this message? You're pathetic!"

At that point, I'd had it. I suddenly blurted out in front of six hundred people, "I don't know what is wrong, but it has not been right here for the past two evenings. Can you please stand and pray with me?"

As we all prayed, God spoke to me—the first time I'd heard His voice in over twenty-four hours. He reminded me of what Paul wrote in 2 Timothy 1:7 and said, "Son, you are intimidated by the worship team on the platform behind you. Break the *spirit of intimidation* and speak what I'm giving you."

I did what He said and a bold message from this scripture immediately followed. It was the most powerful of all twenty-one services. Seventy-five percent of the people came forward, admitting they also battled intimidation. The aisles were packed with people seeking prayer for freedom.

The pastor got back with me a few weeks later to report how effective that service had been. The leaders who'd made the critical comments about me were living in blatant sin—adultery, fornication, and drunkenness. It was all revealed over the next couple of weeks, and all but one left the church. The pastor reported that since then, his worship team had never been so unified and effective. It was a life- and ministry-altering experience.

For me, it ended years of fighting depression and attempting to conduct some services with my God-given gift being inoperative.

The most important discovery was learning that the *spirit of intimidation* must be directly spoken to—no different than Jesus speaking the Word of God directly to Satan during the wilderness temptations. Jesus didn't ask *God* to alleviate the attacks; He addressed the devil, firmly and pointedly, Himself.

ELIJAH'S REPLACEMENT

I encourage you to read 1 Kings 17–19. You will see an experience with intimidation, similar to mine, that Elijah had with Queen Jezebel of Israel.

This great prophet had boldly confronted the nation of Israel on Mount Carmel—an opposition of 850 false prophets, King Ahab, and the royal attendants. Before the entire nation, God had answered Elijah's prayer powerfully with fire. Elijah had even instructed people to execute all the false prophets. Elijah was moving powerfully in his gifting! He then prayed and a three-and-a-half-year drought ended. To top it off, he outran a royal chariot! All of this happened in one day! What a day of ministry!

But before the sun went down, Jezebel heard what had transpired and the real battle began:

> Jezebel sent this message to Elijah: "May the gods strike me and
> even kill me if by this time tomorrow I have not killed you just
> as you killed them." (1 Kings 19:2)

Before commenting on Jezebel's threat, let me say first that spirits are similar to surfers. Surfers need waves to ride on; spirits need words to ride on. We are told, "No weapon turned against you will succeed. *You will silence* every voice raised up to accuse you. These benefits are enjoyed by the servants of the LORD" (Isaiah 54:17). Notice we are to silence every voice raised against us. This is our job, not God's. Jesus didn't ask God to silence Satan in the wilderness. Neither do we when attacked.

Obviously, Jezebel's words carried a massive spirit of intimidation. Once her statement reached Elijah, notice his response: "And when he saw *that*, he arose and ran for his life" (1 Kings 19:3 NKJV).

This man, who had confronted the nation, the false prophets, and the king, now runs away. He traveled the entire length of the nation and went a day's journey into the wilderness, sat down under a tree, and *prayed to die*.

Wow, is this the same person? What is going on? He is obviously confused, depressed, hopeless, and has lost his vision. These are the symptoms of an intimidating spirit. The sad reality is that most people deal with the symptoms instead of addressing the spirit behind them.

In ignorance, I too fought these symptoms for years before that evening God exposed this wicked spirit's ways. I floundered in my gifting and couldn't figure out why.

Elijah had given up, so God sent the dejected prophet on a journey. An angel appeared to him and gave him food for a long forty-day trip to Mount Sinai. Once he arrived, the first thing God asked was, "What are you doing here, Elijah?" (1 Kings 19:9).

What? Hold on! God had instructed the angel to give him food for the trip, so Elijah made the journey. But upon arrival, God asked why he was there. Is God schizophrenic?

No—here is what we must realize. If we are overcome by intimidation, often God will send us to a neutral place to minister to us, because He loves us. I was ignorant of what was transpiring in those meetings, but I don't believe Elijah was. He knew how to boldly confront opposition, but he was scared of this queen.

The real question now becomes: What was behind God's inquiry? God asked why Elijah didn't confront the queen, because she was the one spearheading all the evil. She needed to be stopped, but instead Elijah ran from her.

Rather than responding to the question behind the question, Elijah changed the subject, complaining that he was the only one left truly serving God. It is the classic sob story:

> I have zealously served the LORD God Almighty. But the people
> of Israel have broken their covenant with You, torn down Your
> altars, and killed every one of Your prophets. I am the only one
> left, and now they are trying to kill me, too. (1 Kings 19:10)

God completely ignored this response and once again asked the same question: "What are you doing here, Elijah?" (1 Kings 19:13). And once again, Elijah gave the exact same sob story (see verse 14). He had given up and didn't want to deal with the evil behind the evil.

God once again completely and totally ignored his "woe is me" story and gave the most shocking command:

> Go back the same way you came, and travel to the wilderness
> of Damascus. When you arrive there, anoint Hazael to be king
> of Aram. Then anoint Jehu grandson of Nimshi to be king
> of Israel, and anoint Elisha son of Shaphat from the town of
> Abel-meholah *to replace you as My prophet*. (1 Kings 19:15–16)

Did you take note of the last words, "replace you as My prophet"? God was replacing Elijah because he'd succumbed to, and was overcome by, intimidation. If you continue reading into the second book of Kings, you will find out that Elijah spent the majority of his next four years training his replacement. Also, there's more shocking news: He didn't anoint Hazael or Jehu. His replacement, Elisha, had to do this.

Elisha was not intimidated on any level. He was bold and didn't back down from any wickedness. God says about him, "Those who escape Jehu will be killed by Elisha!" (1 Kings 19:17). Between Jehu and Elisha, the evil dynasty of Ahab and Jezebel was overthrown. I believe that it was originally Elijah's assignment to do this, but due to intimidation, destiny was altered.

We admit that Elijah, unlike the lazy servant, knew the character of God. However, his battle clearly shows what fear and intimidation can do in regard to our gifting and calling.

It's most important to firmly resolve to not back down in the face of fear and intimidation. God will back us when we run up against this force. It is beatable, but we must hit it head-on with God's Word and promises.

I repeat: God is for you. He believes in you. He wants you to flourish in the gifts He's placed in your life. Don't draw back. Don't let anyone or anything deter you from your mission and destiny.

REFLECT

1. Fear has been the thief of many dreams. It's sneaky, seeks to gain control, and if not properly dealt with, it will alter your destiny. In what ways has fear attempted to alter your destiny?

2. Timothy was warned not to neglect his gift. Why is it dangerous to ignore your gift? From the examples listed, what reason for neglect resonated with you the most? Why?

3. Intimidation is a spirit. In what ways have you encountered this spirit? How must this spirit be overcome and defeated?

Make a careful exploration of who you are and the work you have been given, and then sink yourself into that. . . . Each of you must take responsibility for doing the creative best you can with your own life.

—Galatians 6:4–5 MSG

14

Discover and Develop Your Gifts

We now turn to the subject of discovering and developing our God-given gifts. As already stated, it's not my intent to discuss developing natural talents and abilities. With enough practice, almost everyone can become proficient at just about anything.

My family may argue this point when it comes to singing, and they might be right. So, let me cite a realistic example: If I practiced playing a musical instrument for ten thousand hours, I might move from being a terrible musician to an average one. My time and effort might make listening to my playing the piano or guitar enjoyable, but even after all that focused practice, it still would not be a *charisma* that propels my calling to build the kingdom of God.

GOD'S INVOLVEMENT

In the first part of this chapter, we will focus on Paul's words to "make a careful exploration of who you are and the work you have been given." There are no formulas to discover your calling and the accompanying gifts. Even though there are various resources that can help you discover what you're good at, when it comes to making an eternal impact, it takes our Creator's assistance to uncover your *calling* and *charisma*.

At times, God's direct involvement is easy to perceive in the discovery of gifts, such as when He spoke to me to write. I never would have attempted to write if I had not received the word in prayer that summer morning in 1991. No book or course could have convinced me to write, and I definitely wouldn't have stumbled into it. As another example, King David would never have known that he was a warrior if he hadn't protected his sheep from the bear and the lion. After this happened, the need arose for someone to deliver Israel from the Philistines. For David, these previous, threatening predators were just stepping stones to fighting Goliath, as the rest of Israel hid. God allowed David to discover his gifting because of the demanding needs around him.

If you consider Gideon, he was more like me. God needed to convince him through several fleeces that he was called to be a warrior.

Let's begin with square one. It's critical to seek out and believe for God's involvement in discovering your *charisma*. Scripture states that God rewards those who diligently seek Him in faith. It does not say that God rewards those who casually seek Him in wonder and doubt (author's paraphrase of Hebrews 11:6). Along the same lines, Jesus tells us to:

> Keep on asking, and you will receive what you ask for. Keep on seeking, and you will find. Keep on knocking, and the door will be opened to you. For everyone who asks, receives. Everyone who seeks, finds. And to everyone who knocks, the door will be opened. (Matthew 7:7–8)

We must have a passionate desire to know our *charisma*. Hopefully, this book is fueling a burning desire in you to discover and engage your giftings. This longing will prevent you from a nonchalant asking, seeking, or knocking, and instead you will be persistent, as Jesus prescribes above. It's not that God's holding out on you. He wants a passion developed in you for what you're asking for.

In high school, I wanted a high-power telescope because I loved astronomy and wanted to study the night sky. A good scope was completely out of my price range, but I kept reading astronomy books and magazines. I would check out four or five at a time from the library, go through them during my spare time—sometimes repeatedly, then return them and get more. The reading developed an almost desperate desire for the telescope.

Eventually my passion propelled me to devise an unusual idea to raise money for my dream scope. I was a tennis instructor for a swim and racquet club and only gave lessons during summer vacation. I did something that was never done at our club. With the permission of the club's board, I came up with a plan to offer private lessons after school in the fall season. If this worked, I would bring in enough money to buy the telescope. It did! Believe me; I never took that scope for granted. If someone had just given it to me before my desire became so intense, I might have shunned it after the excitement wore off.

God is not hard of hearing. He is not holding out. He desires that you not take for granted the gifts He gives you to build up His people. Your passion needs to be stronger than the adversity you face while on the way to your dreams. So let the desire grow, and the spontaneity will keep you fervently seeking to know your *charisma* and giftings.

Next, we must realize that there is not a patterned way that God answers us; for each child, it's different. It puzzles me sometimes how we continually talk about having a "personal relationship" with Jesus, but when it comes to hearing God, in this case understanding our *charisma* or gifts, we want a formula. God wants to keep it personal. He wants to keep it special between you and Him. He doesn't answer each of His precious children's prayers the exact same way. This is why Jesus instructs us to keep on asking, seeking, and knocking. There is a "searching out" of His will that is actually very good for us.

In our pursuit we should ask ourselves—and others—questions. This is all part of the searching process. We are not looking for the wisdom of man, but to hear God's voice within the voices of those we speak with.

It is important that we know whom to talk to. We must find those who are encouraging, but yet not afraid to speak the truth. I would like to say that these people are in abundance, but they're rare. I know people whom I can go to who will always tell me what I want to hear. Then there are those who are pessimistic, critical, and negative of seemingly everything—they lack vision. Avoid both. Find the person who has faith and is mature and wise. Find a father or mother in the faith, or a wise one who has traveled the journey longer than you and has made mistakes and learned from them.

It's important that those you confide in have avoided becoming jaded or cynical, because these contemptuously distrustful attitudes are fostered in those who harbor offense. Look for a person who's quick to forgive, someone who doesn't get stuck in rote religion but rather progresses with the times and the fresh movements of God's Spirit. Most importantly, it must be someone who sees things from an eternal perspective. When you find this person, do all you can to maintain and treasure the relationship.

There are many who are wise to the world but lack the eternal view. You can only trust their advice to a certain level. Be careful when listening to them, and always filter their advice through the Word of God and prayer.

Parents, a spouse, and pastors all should have your best interest at heart and usually give wise counsel, although there are exceptions.

As a young man, I shared my dreams with my dad about being in the ministry. His generation was a stickler for doing it the "safe way" (which is a weakness when it comes to a life of faith). My dad said, "Son, there is no security in this path." He suggested engineering because I was good in math and science, and he too was an engineer for forty years. It was a safe career choice. I did not realize I was signing up for six years of misery in college and at my first job! Even though I was gifted in these subjects, I was miserable because it wasn't God's call on my life.

My first job as an engineer was working for IBM. One day my boss pulled me into his office and said, "Bevere, what are you doing in engineering? You are a people person; you should be in some field that involves interacting with people." Well-known ministers also pulled me aside in numerous meetings and said, "Son, I see the call of God on you to preach the gospel."

In my alone time in prayer, God continually drew my heart to ministry, even though I wanted nothing to do with it. All the ministers I'd ever met seemed strange. But my heart was still sensitive to our Creator. Before I was saved, I went to a Catholic seminary for a week and I did feel as though I was called to ministry. But it scared me that, as a Catholic priest, I would never be married.

But over and over I continued receiving confirmation, which ultimately helped me put my dad's advice aside. I respected him so much, which pleased God, but I knew something was terribly off as I studied and eventually worked as an engineer. Since I had been repeatedly asking and searching for God's direction, He would not permit me to be misdirected (even by my own well-meaning dad) and made His will abundantly clear.

When it was settled for me, I now had a burning passion that resulted from over a year and a half of searching. I was also three-quarters of the way through getting my engineering degree. I decided to finish and pursue the ministry once I graduated. It was a good decision, as I learned strategies that Bible school wouldn't have taught me. *God will use all experiences to train us!*

Another very important element to discovering your gift is to be planted in a healthy local church. Scripture states, "Those who are *planted* in the house of the LORD shall *flourish*" (Psalm 92:13 NKJV). If you plant a cotton seed, you will not get pumpkins growing out of the soil. The soil is a healthy local church, and when you're committed, your God-given gifts will manifest there. It doesn't matter if you are called to the marketplace, education, government, athletics, or any other field—you will flourish. It's God's design.

QUESTIONS TO ASK YOURSELF
AND WISE FRIENDS

Let's turn our focus to asking questions, both of yourself and wise friends. The right questions asked of the right people may help awaken recognition of what you're gifted to do. Here are some examples.

What Are You Naturally Good At?

This is a good starting place. Perhaps your gift is to understand numbers, eloquently construct sentences, build things, create video stories, design clothes, or organize events. You may have natural athletic abilities, a nose for scents, or an eye for detail. Whatever it is, identify your strengths.

If you're able to hold a tune and have a desire to lead people into the presence of God, this could be a good indicator that you might be called to worship or be involved with some other type of music ministry. The same would be true if you're interested in the human body and find yourself fascinated by medicine. You definitely should ask

God if you are called to healthcare. The list is endless.

But these clues should not be the final word. I was a very good tennis player, started on a team at an NCAA Division I school, and played the USTA circuit and Junior Davis Cup. As already stated, I was a tennis teaching professional for three years and also won the West Virginia state high school tennis tournament. But in prayer, I knew professional tennis wasn't my calling.

On the other hand, I have a friend, Aaron Baddeley, who's an outstanding golfer and is on the PGA Tour. But in 2004—his second year on tour—he was struggling. (He barely requalified to return in 2005 because of finishing 124th on the list.) Near the end of his tough year, while playing in a tournament, he was staying at our house and, sadly, he missed the cut. Together, we got on a plane and went to Las Vegas, where I was scheduled to minister at a conference. In that service, God spoke to his heart four times: "I did not call you to ministry; I called you to golf."

Aaron had been resisting giving his complete efforts in golf, because he wanted to do what I did. He wanted to travel and speak at conferences and churches half-time and play golf half-time. He settled it in his heart that evening that he would give himself fully to his calling and gift. Within a couple of years, he was number sixteen in the world golf rankings and eventually won four PGA Tour events and the Australian Masters. He's been on tour over fifteen years and is still going. His influence has grown, and he has had multiple opportunities to minister and share messages with many who would not have walked through the doors of a church.

I have a pastor friend, Al, who years ago had a man in his church who loved to teach the Bible and was good at it. He wanted to be a teaching pastor. He was also uniquely gifted to fix cars. He was promised a pastoral teaching position in a large church in a different part of the city. He took Pastor Al to lunch to inform him of this. Al is wise and shared with the man, "In praying for you, I don't feel you are called to teach the Bible on a full-time basis. You are exceptionally gifted to work on cars."

The man didn't listen to his pastor's counsel and left for the other church.

A year later, the man was miserable. The teaching position still had not been officially offered to him, his marriage was on the decline, and he was struggling financially. In church one Sunday, the Lord spoke to him: "I never called you to be a pastor, but a mechanic who taught the Bible in your local church."

The man returned to Pastor Al, repented of not listening to his counsel, and came back to his home church. He refocused on his business of fixing cars.

One evening God gave the man a dream of hooking a computer up to a car to diagnose engine problems. He had a friend who understood computers, and the two of them built a computerized diagnostic testing device. It turned out that this testing device could identify problems with cars in a quarter of the time as normal methods. In time, this man opened up garages all over North Carolina with his unique invention. Later, the man walked up to Pastor Al, smiled, and said, "I'm called to fix cars!"

What Energizes You?

One day my assistant asked me to keep a record of "energy levels" for my normal weekly work routine. She set up this rating scale: Those tasks that drained my energy would receive a -2; those that drained minute amounts of energy as a -1; those things that added minimal energy as a +1; and, finally, those things that strongly energized me as a +2.

There were several tasks, such as department meetings, travel, paperwork, packing for trips, and so forth, which got -2 and -1s. A few got +1s, but the only two things that I honestly could score a +2 on were speaking and writing. I was surprised by the results.

In contemplating these findings, I realized that often when I'm writing, I completely lose track of time. There are times I start writing early in the morning and don't realize it's become afternoon. I'm usually mentally tired after so much writing, but I'm also energized.

The same thing happens when preaching. Back in the days when we didn't have time constraints, I would often find myself preaching for more than two hours. It seemed to me like thirty minutes, but I don't know what my audiences thought!

I've watched our creative son, Alec, work on innovative projects for hours with a total loss of awareness of time. He has excelled in our creative department. I've watched Lisa interact with ladies for hours after her women's meetings and lose all concept of time. She is energized by nurturing conversations.

Albert Einstein worked for hours and hours at a time. When he was physically exhausted, he would grab a metal tray and sit in a chair holding the tray in his hands by his knees. Just before he hit deep sleep, the tray would slip out of his hands and hit the floor. The loud crashing sound would awaken him, and he would get back to work.

This is a fairly easy way to determine your calling: Your true gifting will actually energize you, even though you may become mentally or physically tired during long stints. For those who have discovered their true gifting, hours of practice, competing, or working can seem like minutes. So ask yourself, "What is it that energizes me and periodically causes me to lose track of time?"

Your answer is a good indication of where your gifting lies.

What Are You Drawn To?

What grabs your interest? What is it that causes you to come alive? When you sing, is your heart full? Do you find yourself singing when no one else is? I know when I sing, it is a complete labor for me and tires me quickly. It's not my gifting. I couldn't sit in a room and harmonize and write music with others. I have no interest in doing this, but there are people I know who love this.

What magazines interest you? What YouTube videos do you get excited about? What stops you when you are going through Pinterest? What subjects were your favorites in school? What books do you gravitate toward when walking through a bookstore?

Here is an important question: What would you be drawn to do if you were never paid for it? Most professional athletes would play their sport even if they weren't paid for it. My dad would sit me down on Saturday mornings and tell me how a steam engine or some other machine worked. I recall one Saturday morning he spent over an hour drawing and explaining a boiler and how it worked. This would bore me to tears, and I should have figured out then that my calling was not to be an engineer! I loved my dad so much that I never had the heart to tell him I hated those sessions. I made the huge mistake of pursuing engineering to seek financial security—don't make the same error.

How many people are miserable in their job because they do it for one reason—to get a paycheck?

As I mentioned earlier, years ago when my pastor's wife told me they couldn't afford me, my response was, "Oh, yes, you can!" I was willing to work for lower pay, because I was drawn to this type of ministry. Once on the job, the seventy hours a week of serving my pastor and his guests seemed like nothing. I often commented to Lisa that I should be paying my pastors for allowing me to serve them instead of them paying us.

I hesitate to write this, because there's a risk that you may think I'm bragging, but I hope you choose to believe that my motive is to be helpful. When we first started the ministry, Lisa and I decided that my royalties for writing would go to Messenger International. I've now written over twenty books and each one averages between 400 and 450 hours of time to write and edit. This means that I've invested almost nine thousand hours in writing. That's over three years of writing eight hours a day, including the weekends. In essence, I've not been paid for those three years. I've done it because it is my gifting that enhances my calling.

I can honestly say that if I had to choose between doing this and being paid $200,000 per year as an engineer, I would do this again in a heartbeat. This is why the apostle Paul writes:

> I am entrusted with the stewardship of the gospel whether or not I'm paid. So then, where is my reward? It is found in continually depositing the good news into people's hearts, without obligation, free of charge, and not insisting on my rights to be financially supported. (1 Corinthians 9:17–18 TPT)

Who Are You Drawn To?

Recognizing who you're drawn to also reveals a lot about your calling and gifts. Certain people awaken and unlock the gifts within you. Find your tribe—those who share similar giftings and callings as you. They will become pivotal in understanding who you are and how God has gifted you. Your tribe should be people who accept and understand you.

I love sitting with other ministers and discussing adventures and challenges of ministry and, of course, the Word of God. I also love sitting with entrepreneurs and businesspeople. These are all areas of strength in my life.

Running a ministry organization has many similarities with running a marketplace business. Lisa and I have had to be entrepreneurs. When we were young, there were no known ministries quite like what we wanted to do; none that we could pattern ourselves after. We had to blaze a trail. For this reason, entrepreneurs in the business world have always awakened things in me that help me, in a more proficient way, do what we are called to do.

If you love interior design, you will find yourself comfortable around other designers. If you are a doctor, you'll be stimulated by conversing with other physicians. If you are a musician, other musicians will help stir up your gift. I could go on and on; finding your tribe can help you identify, and even draw out, your gifting.

Again, it's important to remember, none of the answers to these questions can ever stand alone and apart from your personal time of seeking God for what He's specifically called you to do. If I had listened to the majority of the ministers who spoke to me in my formative years, I would have picked a city and started a church as a pastor. Very few could see the unique and different callings and gifts that were on Lisa and me. On the other hand, there were a handful of wise ones who helped steer us in the direction we felt in our heart.

DEVELOP YOUR GIFT

Now let's turn our attention to the second half of our opening verse: "Each of you must take responsibility for doing the creative best you can with your own life" (Galatians 6:5 MSG). God has given each of us the potential to build our life, which helps build His kingdom. However, at one time or another, we all have to face the fact that it's not enough to merely possess potential—it must be realized.

How sad would it be for you or me to come to the end of our life knowing we still had more to contribute? At the judgment seat, the pain of regret would be unbearable as we learn what could have been—or worse, the lives that were never impacted because of our negligence to develop what God had entrusted to us.

Settle it now—that you'll die empty, holding nothing back. You will have poured out everything in you so that you're empty. *The world needs what you have—your God-given gifts.*

An interesting insight of the reality of our God-given gifts is found in Proverbs 18:16:

> A man's gift makes room for him,
> And brings him before great men. (NKJV)

Your gift "makes room" for you and brings you before "important people." To "make room" means, "to create space." The "space" we're talking about here is twofold. First, your gift makes room for you to fulfill your potential—bridging the space between *where you are* and *where you could be.* Second, your gift makes room for you to be promoted to new levels of your destiny. Keep in mind that with every promotion, a higher standard of skill is required. Again, Solomon writes:

> If you are uniquely gifted in your work, you will rise and be
> promoted. You won't be held back. (Proverbs 22:29 TPT)

Consider David. In 1 Samuel 16 we find the account of King Saul being tormented by an evil spirit, because the Spirit of the Lord had departed from him. Desperate for relief, Saul ordered his servants to seek out a skilled musician to be brought to him.

One of the young servants responded, "I have seen a son of Jesse the Bethlehemite who plays *skillfully*" (1 Samuel 16:18 AMPC). David wasn't just a *gifted* musician; he was a *skilled* one. What made him *skilled*? His gift was developed, and therefore room was made for him to advance in his calling.

Could it be that many are not progressing in their calling because their gifts are underdeveloped? Could the degree to which our gifts are developed determine the extent to which we *can be* promoted?

Let's return to Paul's words to Timothy that we quoted in the previous chapter. But this time we'll continue on to his suggested remedy for his spiritual son:

> Do not neglect the gift which is in you, [that special inward endowment] which was directly imparted to you . . . *Practice* and *cultivate* and *meditate* upon these duties; *throw yourself wholly into them* [as your ministry], so that your *progress may be evident* to everybody. (1 Timothy 4:14–15 AMPC)

There is so much to learn from these wise words. We observe men and women who excel in their field. Sometimes it's easy to play off their success by stating, "They were born with a special gift." The fact is that they, just as you, were indeed born with a gift, and they chose to develop it. In other words, just because we don't witness them perfecting their gift doesn't mean they haven't worked hard at it.

As mentioned in the previous chapter, Paul begins by warning Timothy to not *neglect* his God-given gift. We neglect our gift by giving little attention to it. Timothy is told that his progress would become evident by fully investing in his gift's development, which Paul wrote would be accomplished through *practice*, *cultivation*, and *meditation*. Let's briefly examine each of these.

Practice

To practice means "to perform or work at repeatedly so as to become proficient," according to Merriam-Webster. Private practice determines our public performance, because we'll always perform according to the level in which we've practiced. It's easy to marvel at a spectacular public performance but lose sight of the weeks, months, and years of training and hard work that went into this level of consistent practice.

According to experts in the science of human behavior and performance, it takes approximately ten thousand hours of practice to become proficient or to master a particular skill. However, Professor K. Anders Ericsson of Florida State University challenges traditional beliefs that "practice makes perfect." The professor takes it a step further by revealing that it's not enough to practice for ten thousand hours unless those hours of practice are done with focused intention to improve, rather than just going through the motions. He coined this type of practice as "purposeful practice." He wrote:

> So here we have purposeful practice in a nutshell: Get outside
> your comfort zone but do it in a focused way, with clear goals,
> a plan for reaching those goals, and a way to monitor your
> progress.[21]

Unless we push ourselves beyond our level of comfort and skill, we'll never grow. If we aren't "purposeful," the danger is that once we reach a level of "good enough," we can easily become complacent. Then it's only a matter of time before we become sloppy in our practice, which will ultimately have a negative effect on our performance and hinder further multiplication.

Developing your area of strength is liberating, not limiting. It increases your potential to multiply. This does not mean that we don't work on areas of weakness or acquire new skills; it means we're focused and invested in the areas that will yield the greatest return on our potential.

I recommend learning new skills, but never at the neglect of your areas of calling.

Here's the bottom line: Growth is not automatic; it requires intentionality. Unless we're consistently practicing so that we can become "skilled" in our gifts, we'll never realize our full potential. That's why we must remain committed to personal growth. Most people want to do great things with their life, but not everyone is willing to put in the necessary work to become great. Practice is paying the price that produces great rewards.

Cultivate

Practice is practical, while cultivating is more educational. To "cultivate" means, "to develop or improve by education or training; to promote the growth and development of."[22]

When you consider the word *cultivate*, think "coaching." Coaching is critical to your personal growth and development, as it provides constructive criticism and guidance that cannot be acquired on your own. Anyone who has excelled in their gifting has had coaching and guidance from others along their journey. The wonderful element of coaches is that they see your potential and they're committed to drawing it out of you—even if that includes being hard on you!

Coaching can come through mentor-mentee, father-child, mother-child, teacher-student, coaching relationships, apprenticeships, internships, and indirectly from books, courses, and resources that are available to us in abundance.

Another way to receive education in your area of gifting is to gather with those who share similar giftings. Again, as mentioned earlier, this is often referred to as "finding your tribe." When you're in the presence of those who share similar talents and passions, it offers the opportunity to collaborate and innovate together.

During the 1930s and 1940s, a group of creative writers—known as The Inklings—met in a private room in a pub near the grounds of the University of Oxford. Among these literary enthusiasts were C.S. Lewis and J.R.R. Tolkien. The purpose of these gatherings was to read and critique the members' unfinished works—from which were inspired the creation of Tolkien's *The Lord of the Rings* and Lewis's *The Chronicles of Narnia*. Talk about a great tribe!

Meditate

To "meditate" means "to reflect; to contemplate." Certain growth can only occur when we take the time to stop and reflect on the lessons we're learning. When we honestly monitor our growth and allow ourselves time to evaluate our progress and performance, we position ourselves to become aware of the specific areas that need attention or improvement.

My friend John Maxwell often reminds his audiences and readers that experience is not the best teacher—*evaluated experience* is. As you reflect on your progress, take to heart the feedback you receive from coaches and peers, as well as think about innovative ways to improve and utilize your gifts. Ask yourself and God the right questions: What do I need to change? What have been my biggest areas of growth? What are the areas I need to give more attention to? What is required for me to break through to a new level?

Reflection time is never wasted time.

HOLD NOTHING BACK

Finally, let's revisit Paul's words to Timothy:

Practice and cultivate and meditate upon these duties; *throw yourself wholly into them* [as your ministry], so that your progress may be evident to everybody. (1 Timothy 4:15 AMPC)

Everything we've discussed is contingent upon giving ourselves completely to what God has called and gifted us to do. Your calling demands your full commitment. As we give ourselves wholeheartedly to what God has entrusted to us, our progress will become evident to all, and we'll multiply our potential.

Each of us is responsible for stewarding our gifts and doing the creative best we can with our own lives. By now we've seen that the degree to which our gifts are developed will determine the degree to which we can advance in our sphere of calling and multiply our effectiveness.

We have one shot at this life to give it everything we have. Let's hold nothing back, and let's be emptied, pouring ourselves out completely as a gift back to God. This is living. This is when we'll truly come alive and experience life to its fullest.

REFLECT

1. There are no formulas to discover your calling. Even though there are various resources that can help you discover what you're good at, locating your calling and gifts will require God's involvement. Have you sought God for insight into your calling and gifts? What has He shown you?

2. In our pursuit of our calling, we should ask ourselves—and others—questions. This is all part of the process. Find people you trust and ask them what they see on you and in you.

3. It's not enough to merely possess potential—it must be realized. Why is it important that you develop your gifts? What happens when your gifts are intentionally grown and developed?

Now He who establishes us with you in Christ and has anointed us is God.

—2 Corinthians 1:21 NKJV

15

Anointed

During a recent Thanksgiving holiday, our family was sitting around the dining room table. Lisa had made a remarkable feast. We were all basking in its afterglow and enjoying each other's company. I felt that as the dad, I needed to say something to my family, as well as a few of our team members who had joined us.

After I uttered an inward prayer, a word came to my heart: "Guys, I'm now sixty years old and feel, in more ways than one, my father-role responsibility of sharing a bit of wisdom. If you were to ask me what the most important thing that Lisa and I have done in walking with God during the past forty years, it would be this: *Stay consistent*.

"We've had many opportunities over the years to 'throw in the towel,' so to speak. Also, many opportunities to compromise truth for personal gain, self-promotion, or to alleviate a trial we were experiencing. But we've chosen to make truth our anchor, holding on to it no matter how painful the circumstances.

"A very wise statement Job made in his turmoil was, 'I can take comfort in this: Despite the pain, I have not denied the words of the Holy One' (Job 6:10). When I've made mistakes (and I've made a lot of them), I've been quick to repent and ask forgiveness, both with God and man. I look now at the blessings that abound from consistent obedience to truth, and they are mind-blowing. God is so very gracious."

THE ANOINTING

A great blessing that has resulted from consistently submitting to truth is "the anointing." To understand this, let's turn to the great ordination—the day when God the Father inaugurated Jesus as King of heaven and earth:

> For You have cherished righteousness and detested lawlessness.
> *For this reason*, God, Your God, has *anointed You* and poured
> out the oil of bliss on You *more than on any of Your friends.*
> (Hebrews 1:9 TPT)

Pay attention to the words *for this reason,* as they are crucial to understanding a key truth. Jesus's immovability on two issues resulted in a great benefit, and His example should be our standard. Jesus loved *righteousness.* It is the Greek word *dikaiosúnē* and is defined as "conformity to the claims of higher authority."[23] But at the same time, He hated *lawlessness.* There are a lot of Christians who *dislike* lawlessness, but this is not the heart of Jesus: He *hates* it. The Greek word is *anomía,* which in essence means "disobedience to the authority of God." He hated anything to do with departing from God's authority. Period. Jesus's steadfast obedience, no matter the difficulty, was the reason that the anointing on His life was more powerful than that of any of His companions.

Why do I close this book on multiplication discussing *the anointing*? The answer is simple, yet important: *The anointing is what fuels our God-given abilities to eternally multiply.* Think of it as an enhancer to what you are gifted to do. Let me give two quick examples.

I've heard people with tremendous voices that I appreciated, but then I've heard those with less magnificent voices who moved my heart more deeply, which resulted in change. The difference was *the anointing*. I've also heard people utter messages with profound content, while there have been other, less notable messages that affected me deeply at the heart level, which brought behavioral change. The difference was *the anointing*.

The same effect is true for all God's servants, no matter the field of calling, whether it's government, business, the arts, education, and so forth. King David made this statement:

> But my horn (emblem of excessive strength and stately grace)
> You have exalted like that of a wild ox; I am *anointed* with fresh
> oil. (Psalm 92:10 AMPC)

His words are so revealing. In examining a few of the leading commentaries on this verse, there is mutual agreement that the emphasis is not the "wild ox" but rather the idea that "You have made me very strong." The anointing brings joy. God calls it *the oil of bliss* or *joy*, which according to Scripture is our *strength* (see Nehemiah 8:10). In essence, the psalmist declares that the anointing makes us strong. It enhances and strengthens the gifts on our life to bear eternal fruit.

I believe this is one of the unspoken, game-changing aspects of the parable of the talents and minas: The labor of the two multiplying servants was enhanced by the anointing. I say "unspoken" because this truth is gleaned from the aforementioned scriptures. In order for them to multiply, it was important to consistently obey and to hate disobeying the instructions of their master, thus attracting the anointing to enhance their gifts.

David makes mention of the oil being *fresh*. Anointing is not a one-time occurrence, but rather the blessing that begins and continues in one who consistently walks in submission to God. It is not something gained at one point in time and then taken for granted, because now "I've got it." Samson had the anointing but didn't keep it fresh. He compromised and disobeyed; he didn't hate lawlessness. He got away with it a few times, but eventually his sin caught up to him. Scripture states:

> *His strength left him.* And she [Delilah] said, "The Philistines are upon you, Samson!" So he awoke from his sleep, and said, "I will go out as before, at other times, and shake myself free!" But *he did not know* that the LORD had departed from him. (Judges 16:19–20 NKJV)

Samson was unaware that the anointing had lifted. This is why David, after his disobedience in regard to Bathsheba, passionately prays:

> Create in me a clean heart, O God. Renew a *loyal* spirit within me. Do not banish me from Your presence, and don't take your Holy Spirit from me. Restore to me the *joy* of Your salvation, and make me *willing to obey* You. (Psalm 51:10–12)

David's heart cry, his great plea, was that the anointing would not be removed from his life, and he knew it would depend on a loyal or a *consistent* life of obedience to God.

Let's continue to examine the anointing and to whom it's given. Look again at Paul's statement highlighted at the opening of this chapter:

> Now He who establishes us with you in Christ and has *anointed us* is God. (2 Corinthians 1:21 NKJV)

The word for "anointed" here in the Greek is *chríō*. It is defined as "to assign a person to a task, with the implication of supernatural *sanctions*, blessing, and endowment—'to anoint, to assign, to *appoint.*'"[24]

There are key words here that cannot be overlooked. The word *sanction* is defined as "authoritative permission or approval, as for an action." Simply put, the anointing is the *divine approval to act*. Jesus states, "The Spirit of the Lord is upon me, for He has *anointed me to* . . ." (Luke 4:18). The anointing was God's approval upon Jesus *to do* something. Again, in the same manner the apostle Peter states, "God *anointed* Jesus of Nazareth with the Holy Spirit and with power, who went about *doing* . . ." (Acts 10:38 NKJV). Again, it's for action.

Another key component of *chríō* are the defining words *assign or appoint*. In serving God, there is always a testing period. We are tested in obedience before we are appointed, or anointed.

With the story of Mike I mentioned in chapter 9, his critical test occurred when God asked him to give his last $200. In regard to Lisa and me, our test was whether we would stay committed to the divine directive to write—even when no publishers were interested in our first two books, and there was very low interest from the general public.

Jesus says more than once, "'Many are called, but few chosen'" (Matthew 20:16 and 22:14 NKJV). I believe the word *many* references all who belong to Him. Each of us has a divine calling. However, the word *chosen* means "appointed" and, according to Jesus, that number, sadly, is "few." Why? There is an approval process that must be passed. Read these words carefully: "Greet Apelles, that one *tried* and *approved* in Christ" (Romans 16:10 AMPC).

Apelles was put on trial, as are all of us who desire to journey toward our destiny. He obviously passed the test and therefore was *chosen* or *approved*. From the principles of the Scripture we know, without being told, that Apelles was anointed, because his gifting had the enhanced touch of God upon it.

There are so many who prematurely self-appoint in the actual area they are called to, but it is not their own approval they should strive for, but the divine approval:

For [it is] not [the man] who praises *and* commends himself who is approved *and* accepted, but [it is the person] whom the Lord accredits *and* commends. (2 Corinthians 10:18 AMPC)

Let's circle back to the Thanksgiving dinner. I wanted my family and team members who were present to know that *consistent obedience*—loving righteousness and hating lawlessness—is crucial to the fulfillment of our destiny, because such consistency positions us for His anointing.

In looking back over our lives, Lisa and I have obeyed God in some very difficult times: often this obedience appeared counterproductive, even detrimental, to our growth, well-being, popularity, or many other personal benefits we were seemingly walking away from. But what looked to be disadvantageous to us in the short run, actually ended up being the very key that opened a significant door to our destiny.

YOUR COMMISSION

You are called as much as anyone—including even your greatest heroes of the faith. More than likely, your calling is not in the organized church world, because only some—a small number—are called to this sphere. You are privileged to excel, to stand out in the arena of life you're sent to.

- Daniel *distinguished himself* in the government offices of Babylon (see Daniel 6:3 NKJV).
- Joseph *distinguished himself* in the great nation of Egypt (See Genesis 41:39).
- Phoebe *stood out* as a minister of the gospel in Cenchrea (See Romans 16:1).
- Your calling is no different.

You are uniquely gifted. God has placed on you the abilities required to fulfill your mission.

Listen to Scripture's record of Bezalel and his team of workers: "The LORD has gifted Bezalel, Oholiab, and the other *skilled* craftsmen with *wisdom* and *ability* to perform any task involved in building the sanctuary" (Exodus 36:1). These men didn't possess the ability, like Moses or Aaron and his sons, to speak the Word of God and minister to the people. But these craftsmen were gifted to work with their hands to build the tabernacle.

You too have been gifted to build God's tabernacle with the skills He's given you. However, this sanctuary isn't made of gold, silver, bronze, precious stones, badgers' skins, fine linen, acacia wood, or any other materials used to build the tabernacle of the Old Testament or the temple in Jerusalem. Today, God's tabernacle is made out of living stones—human beings—and these living stones are being built up as a habitation of God (see 1 Peter 2:5 and Ephesians 2:20–22). You are gifted to build people for God's glory.

You are empowered to multiply. We are stewards of the gifts God gives us, and His desire is for you and me to return to Him multiplied fruit that has been produced by these gifts. To multiply, we must seek out the strategies of heaven. Principles can be taught by leaders, but these unique, heavenly strategies are personal; they aren't studied from a book or learned in a classroom.

We leaders can only encourage you to seek Him and listen to His voice. Obey Him, even when it seems insignificant. What ends up multiplying is usually something that seems trivial. Remember, it is a mustard seed, smaller than all other seeds, that grows into one of the largest trees.

You multiply through investing. This takes on many forms, but when we release, we receive a harvest of blessings. If the seed remains unplanted (uninvested), it remains alone, but when invested, it produces a multiplied harvest. At any point, either your harvest can be hoarded or you can reinvest it. Don't ever stop investing; it is the key to your next level of effectiveness.

Your catalyst is serving. If your motive is anything other than to serve, you will end up in a place where you don't want to find yourself. You may be very well off in the eyes of others, but you will be drained of passion. Your lamp will continue to diminish, even to the point of going out. But, be comforted—He will not quench a smoking lamp. He will continually seek to gain your attention, to rekindle your fire (see Isaiah 42:3). No matter what you do, seek to serve, love without hypocrisy, and endure any hardships you face.

Desire the anointing. It is your enhancer. It will propel your work to become eternal. It will exalt your strength and make you stand out in your field of calling. It will separate you from those in the world— and even in the church—who use their God-given gifts for selfish or worldly purposes.

You must have faith. It is the only way to multiply your God-given potential. Without faith, "it is impossible to please God" (Hebrews 11:6). In order to grow it, you must hear His Word. We are told, "Faith *comes* by hearing, and hearing by the word of God" (Romans 10:17 NKJV). It's hearing, and then hearing, and then hearing again that causes the Word of God to be firmly embedded in our heart. This is why it would be wise to read this book again, and then again. But don't just read it! Put the book down and meditate on how these truths apply to you—then act on them. Get the Word of God, which is systematically laid out in this book, into your spirit through reading, meditation, and prayer to the point that you believe you are called to multiply no matter what life looks like around you. This conviction inside of you to multiply should grow bigger than your outward circumstances would dictate.

Finally remember, *God is for you!* He says:

"For I know the plans I have for you," says the LORD. "They are plans for good." (Jeremiah 29:11)

And again, we are emphatically told:

If God is for us, who can ever be against us? Since He did not spare even His own Son but gave Him up for us all, won't He also give us everything else? (Romans 8:31–32)

Listen to these words, not the discouraging statements that originate from the *god of this world*—the chief accuser and discourager. Your Creator is your Father, and He desires your success in the labor He's called you to.

As a father in the faith, who has now passed his sixtieth year, I'm also for you! I'm cheering you on to go further than my peers and I have gone. We serve one King, are citizens of one kingdom, are members of one household, we have one faith, one mission—to build the house of God that He will inhabit for all eternity.

Let's work together. Let's become one and maintain unity. Let's see His glory fill His dwelling place once again. There is no other solution for the world's problems.

I love you but, most importantly, God the Father, Jesus Christ the Son, and the Holy Spirit deeply love you. And *their love for you endures forever.*

Now to Him Who is able to keep you without stumbling *or* slipping *or* falling, and to present [you] unblemished (blameless and faultless) before the presence of His glory in triumphant joy *and* exultation [with unspeakable, ecstatic delight]—To the one only God, our Savior through Jesus Christ our Lord, be glory (splendor), majesty, might *and* dominion, and power *and* authority, before all time and now and forever (unto all the ages of eternity). Amen (so be it). —Jude 24–25 (AMPC)

REFLECT

1. The anointing is what fuels our God-given abilities to multiply. How is the anointing cultivated? What difference does the anointing make to the outworking of your gifts?

2. How can the anointing remain fresh in your life? What happens if the anointing is taken for granted?

3. What arena of life are you called to in which you will make a difference? In what ways could the anointing distinguish you within that particular sphere of influence?

If you confess with your mouth that Jesus is Lord and believe in your heart that God raised Him from the dead, you will be saved. For it is by believing in your heart that you are made right with God, and it is by confessing with your mouth that you are saved.

—Romans 10:9–10

Appendix

Salvation, Available to All

God wants you to experience life in its fullness. He's passionate about you and the plan He has for your life. But there's only one way to start the journey to your destiny: by receiving salvation through God's Son, Jesus Christ.

Through the death and resurrection of Jesus, God made a way for you to enter His kingdom as a beloved son or daughter. The sacrifice of Jesus on the Cross made eternal and abundant life freely available to you. Salvation is God's gift to you; you cannot do anything to earn or deserve it.

To receive this precious gift, first acknowledge your sin of living independently of your Creator, for this is the root of all the sins you have committed. This repentance is a vital part of receiving salvation. Peter made this clear, on the day that five thousand were saved in the Book of Acts: "Repent therefore and be converted, that your sins may be blotted out" (Acts 3:19 NKJV). Scripture declares that each of us is born a slave to sin. This slavery is rooted in the sin of Adam, who began the pattern of willful disobedience. Repentance is a choice to walk away from obedience to yourself and Satan, the father of lies, and to turn in obedience to your new Master, Jesus Christ—the One who gave His life for you.

You must give Jesus the lordship of your life. To make Jesus

"Lord" means that you give Him ownership of your life (spirit, soul, and body)—everything you are and have. His authority over your life becomes absolute. The moment you do this, God delivers you from darkness and transfers you to the light and glory of His kingdom. You simply go from death to life—you become His child!

If you want to receive salvation through Jesus, pray these words:

God in Heaven, I acknowledge that I am a sinner and have fallen short of Your righteous standard. I deserve to be judged for eternity for my sin. Thank You for not leaving me in this state, for I believe You sent Jesus Christ, Your only begotten Son, who was born of the Virgin Mary, to die for me and carry my judgment on the Cross. I believe He was raised again on the third day and is now seated at Your right hand as my Lord and Savior. So on this day, I repent of my independence from You and give my life entirely to the lordship of Jesus.

Jesus, I confess you as my Lord and Savior. Come into my life through Your Spirit and change me into a child of God. I renounce the things of darkness that I once held on to, and from this day forward I will no longer live for myself. But by Your grace, I will live for You who gave Yourself for me that I may live forever.

Thank You, Lord; my life is now completely in Your hands, and according to Your Word, I shall never be ashamed. In Jesus's name, Amen.

Welcome to the family of God! I encourage you to share your exciting news with another believer. It's also important that you join a Bible-believing local church and connect with others who can encourage you in your new faith. You have just embarked on the most remarkable journey. May you grow in revelation, grace, and friendship with God every day!

ACKNOWLEDGMENTS

The book in your hand is a team effort, so I want to acknowledge some of the coworkers who contributed to it:

Bruce Nygren: Thank you for your expertise in the content editing. Once again, you've taken my writing and, without losing my voice, made it a much better read. And thank you for the challenging questions you asked that ultimately made the book more accurate and stronger.

Cory Emberson, Laura Willbur, and Loran Johnson: Thank you for ensuring that the grammar, punctuation, and style of this message stayed accurate and consistent. I admire your gift.

Chris Pace: Thank you for your unending encouragement in reading this manuscript as it progressed chapter by chapter. Thank you also for helping me shape chapter 14. Your input was invaluable.

Addison Bevere: Thank you for your editing skills and your challenging questions, which made the message a better and more accurate read. Most of all, thank you for being a faithful and encouraging son.

Allan Nygren: Thank you for your brilliant design of the layout of this book and the cover. I admire your gift!

To the Messenger International Team: Each of you does so much behind the scenes to build God's kingdom. I will rejoice with you on the day we witness Jesus greatly reward your selfless service.

Holy Spirit of God: My greatest gratitude goes to You! This message would never have been possible without Your guidance and wisdom. I'm exceedingly thankful for Your ongoing revelation of my Lord and greatest love, Jesus Christ. I love You deeply, and it is an honor to serve You and partner with You.

NOTES

1. Zodhiates, Spiros. *The Complete Word Study Dictionary: New Testament*. Chattanooga, TN: AMG Publishers, 2000.

2. Arndt, William, Frederick W. Danker, and Walter Bauer. *A Greek – English Lexicon of the New Testament and Other Early Christian Literature*. Chicago: University of Chicago Press, 2000.

3. Louw, Johannes P., and Eugene Albert Nida. *Greek – English Lexicon of the New Testament: Based on Semantic Domains*. New York: United Bible Societies, 1996.

4. Louw, Johannes P., and Eugene Albert Nida. *Greek – English Lexicon of the New Testament: Based on Semantic Domains*. New York: United Bible Societies, 1996.

5. Louw, Johannes P., and Eugene Albert Nida. *Greek – English Lexicon of the New Testament: Based on Semantic Domains*. New York: United Bible Societies, 1996, and Zodhiates, Spiros. *The Complete Word Study Dictionary: New Testament*. Chattanooga, TN: AMG Publishers, 2000.

6. Zodhiates, Spiros. *The Complete Word Study Dictionary: New Testament*. Chattanooga, TN: AMG Publishers, 2000.

7. Louw, Johannes P., and Eugene Albert Nida. *Greek – English Lexicon of the New Testament: Based on Semantic Domains*. New York: United Bible Societies, 1996.

8. Zodhiates, Spiros. *The Complete Word Study Dictionary: New Testament*. Chattanooga, TN: AMG Publishers, 2000.

9. Louw, Johannes P., and Eugene Albert Nida. *Greek – English Lexicon of the New Testament: Based on Semantic Domains*. New York: United Bible Societies, 1996.

10. Louw, Johannes P., and Eugene Albert Nida. *Greek – English Lexicon of the New Testament: Based on Semantic Domains*. New York:

United Bible Societies, 1996.

11. "Enthusiasm." Merriam-Webster.com. Accessed March 18, 2020. https://www.merriam-webster.com/dictionary/enthusiasm.

12. "Breakthrough." Dictionary.com. Accessed May 5, 2020. https://www.dictionary.com/browse/breakthrough.

13. Baker, Warren, and Eugene E. Carpenter. *The Complete Word Study Dictionary: Old Testament*. Chattanooga, TN: AMG Publishers, 2003.

14. Zodhiates, Spiros. *The Complete Word Study Dictionary: New Testament*. Chattanooga, TN: AMG Publishers, 2000.

15. https://www.barna.com/research/digital-babylon/. Accessed January 10, 2020.

16. Zodhiates, Spiros. *The Complete Word Study Dictionary: New Testament*. Chattanooga, TN: AMG Publishers, 2000.

17. Louw, Johannes P., and Eugene Albert Nida. *Greek – English Lexicon of the New Testament: Based on Semantic Domains*. New York: United Bible Societies, 1996.

18. Myles Munroe, *Maximizing Your Potential* Expanded Edition, Kindle. Shippensburg, PA: Destiny Image, 2013, 145.

19. Zodhiates, Spiros. *The Complete Word Study Dictionary: New Testament*. Chattanooga, TN: AMG Publishers, 2000.

20. Arndt, William, Frederick W. Danker, Walter Bauer, and F. Wilbur Gingrich. *A Greek—English Lexicon of the New Testament and Other Early Christian Literature*. Chicago: University of Chicago Press, 2000.

21. Anders Ericsson, *Peak: Secrets from the New Science of Expertise*. New York: Houghton Mifflin Harcourt, 2016, 22.

22. "Cultivate." Dictionary.com. Accessed February 1, 2020. https://www.dictionary.com/browse/cultivate.

23. Zodhiates, Spiros. *The Complete Word Study Dictionary: New Testament*. Chattanooga, TN: AMG Publishers, 2000.

24. Louw, Johannes P., and Eugene Albert Nida. *Greek – English Lexicon of the New Testament: Based on Semantic Domains*. New York: United Bible Societies, 1996.

MULTIPLY YOUR
GOD-GIVEN POTENTIAL

STAY ENGAGED WITH
JOHN BEVERE

#XMULTIPLYBOOK | JOHNBEVERE.COM

Introducing

MessengerX

Now you can access our entire
library of discipleship content!
Download the app at no cost today.

Scan the QR code to download MessengerX

MessengerX.com

BOOKS BY JOHN

A Heart Ablaze

The Bait of Satan*

Breaking Intimidation*

Drawing Near

Driven by Eternity*

Enemy Access Denied

Extraordinary

The Fear of the Lord

God, Where Are You?!*

Good or God?*

The Holy Spirit: An Introduction*

Honor's Reward*

How to Respond When You Feel Mistreated

Killing Kryptonite*

Relentless*

Rescued

The Story of Marriage*

Thus Saith the Lord?

Under Cover*

The Voice of One Crying

Available in study or course format

Messenger International exists to develop uncompromising followers of Christ who transform our world.

If you want to learn more about how you can get involved with Messenger International, we'd love to connect with you.

Call: **1-800-648-1477**

Visit us online at: **MessengerInternational.org**